What people are saying

"Here at Citibank we use the Quick Course® computer training book series for 'just-in-time' job aids—the books are great for users who are too busy for tutorials and training. Quick Course® books provide very clear instruction and easy reference."

Bill Moreno, Development Manager
Citibank
San Francisco, CA

"At Geometric Results, much of our work is PC related and we need training tools that can quickly and effectively improve the PC skills of our people. Early this year we began using your materials in our internal PC training curriculum and the results have been outstanding. Both participants and instructors like the books and the measured learning outcomes have been very favorable."

Roger Hill, Instructional Systems Designer
Geometric Results Incorporated
Southfield, MI

"The concise and well organized text features numbered instructions, screen shots, and useful quick reference pointers, and tips…[This] affordable text is very helpful for educators who wish to build proficiency."

Computer Literacy column
Curriculum Administrator Magazine
Stamford, CT

"I have purchased five other books on this subject that I've probably paid more than $60 for, and your [Quick Course®] book taught me more than those five books combined!"

Emory Majors
Searcy, AR

"I would like you to know how much I enjoy the Quick Course® books I have received from you. The directions are clear and easy to follow with attention paid to every detail of the particular lesson."

Betty Weinkauf, Retired Senior
Mission, TX

QUICK COURSE®

in

MICROSOFT®
POWERPOINT
97

ONLINE PRESS INC.

Microsoft Press

PUBLISHED BY
Microsoft Press
A Division of Microsoft Corporation
One Microsoft Way
Redmond, WA 98052-6399

Library of Congress Cataloging-in-Publication Data

Quick Course in Microsoft PowerPoint 97 / Online Press Inc.
     p.   cm.
   Includes index.
   ISBN 1-57231-724-8
   1. Computer graphics.   2. Microsoft PowerPoint (Computer file)
 I. Online Press Inc.
 T385.Q53 1997
 006.6'869--dc21   97-27393
                                                  CIP

Printed and bound in the United States of America.

1 2 3 4 5 6 7 8 9 QMQM 2 1 0 9 8 7

Distributed to the book trade in Canada by Macmillan of Canada, a division of Canada Publishing Corporation.

A CIP record of this book is available from the British Library.

Microsoft Press books are available through booksellers and distributors worldwide. For further information about international editions, contact your local Microsoft Corporation office. Or contact Microsoft Press International directly at fax (425) 936-7329. Visit our Web site at mspress.microsoft.com.

A Quick Course® Education/Training Edition for this title is published by Online Press Inc. For information about supplementary workbooks, contact Online Press Inc. at 14320 NE 21st St., Suite 18, Bellevue, WA, 98007, USA, 1-800-854-3344.

Authors: Joyce Cox and Polly Urban of Online Press Inc., Bellevue, Washington
Acquisitions Editor: Susanne M. Freet
Project Editor: Maureen Williams Zimmerman

From the publisher

"I love these books!"

I can't tell you the number of times people have said those exact words to me about our new Quick Course® software training book series. And when I ask them what makes the books so special, this is what they say:

- **They're short and approachable, but they give you hours worth of good information.**

  Written for busy people with limited time, most Quick Course books are designed to be completed in 15 to 40 hours. Because Quick Course books are usually divided into two parts—Learning the Basics and Building Proficiency—users can selectively choose the chapters that meet their needs and complete them as time allows.

- **They're relevant and fun, and they assume you're no dummy.**

  Written in an easy-to-follow, step-by-step format, Quick Course books offer streamlined instruction for the new user in the form of no-nonsense, to-the-point tutorials and learning exercises. Each book provides a logical sequence of instructions for creating useful business documents—the same documents people use on the job. People can either follow along directly or substitute their own information and customize the documents. After finishing a book, users have a valuable "library" of documents they can continually recycle and update with new information.

- **They're direct and to the point, and they're a lot more than just pretty pictures.**

  Training-oriented rather than feature-oriented, Quick Course books don't cover the things you don't really need to know to do useful work. They offer easy-to-follow, step-by-step instructions; lots of screen shots for checking work in progress; quick-reference pointers for fast, easy lookup and review; and useful tips offering additional information on topics being discussed.

- **They're a rolled-into-one-book solution, and they meet a variety of training needs.**

  Designed with instructional flexibility in mind, Quick Course books can be used both for self-training and as the basis for weeklong courses, two-day seminars, and all-day workshops. They can be adapted to meet a variety of training needs, including classroom instruction, take-away practice exercises, and self-paced learning.

Microsoft Press is very excited about bringing you this extraordinary series. But you must be the judge. I hope you'll give these books a try. And maybe the next time I see you, you too will say, "Hey, Jim! I love these books!"

Jim Brown, Publisher
Microsoft Press

Content overview

Content details

PART ONE: LEARNING THE BASICS

PART TWO: BUILDING PROFICIENCY

ONE

LEARNING THE BASICS

In Part One, we cover basic techniques for working with Microsoft PowerPoint. After you have completed these three chapters, you will know enough to be able to create and deliver simple presentations. In Chapter 1, you learn how to work with the program while creating a simple presentation using the AutoContent Wizard, and you learn the basics of presentation delivery. In Chapter 2, you start a new presentation based on a design template and tackle editing and formatting. Finally, in Chapter 3, you use separate programs to create graphs, organization charts, and tables to visually represent data on your slides.

1 Creating a Simple Presentation

We use the AutoContent Wizard to get started and then show you how to edit slides. Next we cover the basics of delivering a presentation, including the creation of overheads, speaker's notes, and handouts. Finally, we show you how to get help and how to quit PowerPoint.

We edited sample text provided by the AutoContent Wizard to create this presentation. We then ran the presentation as an electronic slide show and produced overheads and 35mm slides.

Paranormal Tours

Lilly Peushin
Gulliver's Travel Incorporated

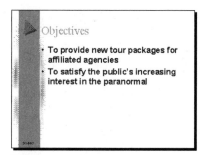

Objectives

- To provide new tour packages for affiliated agencies
- To satisfy the public's increasing interest in the paranormal

Customer Requirements

- Tours that are not only insightful but enjoyable
- Tours that focus on the latest developments in paranormalism
- Tour packages that are flexible

Some Sample Tours

- Ghostly Bed & Breakfasts
  - Europe
  - United States
- Mythical Monsters
- Extraterrestrial Exploration

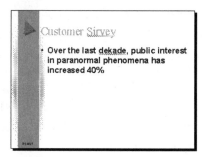

Customer Sirvey

- Over the last dekade, public interest in paranormal phenomena has increased 40%

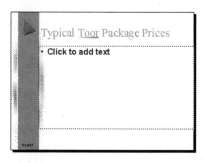

Typical Toor Package Prices

- Click to add text

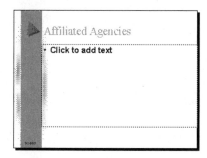

Affiliated Agencies

- Click to add text

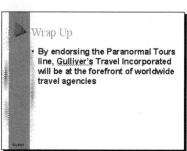

Wrap Up

- By endorsing the Paranormal Tours line, Gulliver's Travel Incorporated will be at the forefront of worldwide travel agencies

Other ways to start PowerPoint

Instead of starting PowerPoint by choosing it from the Start menu, you can create a shortcut icon for PowerPoint on your Windows 95 desktop. Right-click an open area of the desktop and choose New and then Shortcut from the object menu. In the Create Shortcut dialog box, click the Browse button, navigate to Program Files\Microsoft Office\Microsoft PowerPoint, and click Next. Then type a name for the shortcut icon and click Finish. (To delete a shortcut icon, simply drag it to the Recycle Bin.) For maximum efficiency, you can start PowerPoint and open an existing presentation by choosing Documents from the Start menu and then choosing the presentation from the Documents submenu, where Windows 95 stores the names of up to 15 of the most recently opened files. If you are using Microsoft Office and have installed the Office shortcut bar, you can click the Open Office Document button on the shortcut bar and navigate to the folder in which the presentation you want to open is stored, or you can choose Open Office Document from the top of the Start menu. To start PowerPoint and open a new presentation, click the New Office Document button found on the Office shortcut bar or choose New Office Document from the top of the Start menu.

If we conducted a survey of people who use computers as part of their jobs, we would probably find that most of the survey respondents work with one or two programs most of the time, with another couple of programs every so often, and with a few programs once in a blue moon. And of the respondents who have some kind of presentation program installed on their computers, most would put that program in the second or, more likely, the third category. Very few people develop presentations for a living, and for most people, developing presentations is not a big enough part of their jobs to warrant spending hours becoming an expert.

Fortunately, sophisticated presentation packages like Microsoft PowerPoint provide a lot of support for occasional users. If we are suddenly faced with the task of creating a presentation—for example, to present a new product to the company's salespeople—we can focus on the message of the presentation and leave the aesthetic details to PowerPoint. In fact, as you'll see in this chapter, PowerPoint can even help us structure the content of the presentation so that we can successfully get our message across.

Throughout this book, we focus on how to use PowerPoint to produce simple yet effective presentations, and for our examples, we show you how to create presentations for a travel agency. You will easily be able to adapt these examples to your particular needs. Because adequate planning and smooth delivery are essential if you want your presentations to have maximum impact, we weave these topics into the chapters where appropriate. By the time you have worked your way through this book, you'll know not only how to use Power-Point but how to develop and deliver a presentation that accomplishes your goals.

We assume that you have already installed both Windows 95 and PowerPoint 97 on your computer. We also assume that you've worked with Windows 95 before and that you know how to start programs, move windows, choose commands from menus, highlight text, and so on. If you are a new Windows user, we suggest you take a look at *Quick Course*®

in Windows 95, another book in our series, which will help you come up to speed.

It's time to get started, so let's fire up PowerPoint:

1. Choose Programs and then Microsoft PowerPoint from the Windows 95 Start menu.

Starting PowerPoint

2. If the Office Assistant appears, click the Start Using Microsoft PowerPoint option to close the assistant. (We'll discuss the Office Assistant in more detail on page 29.) PowerPoint then displays this dialog box:

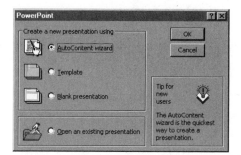

As you can see, you can start a new presentation in one of three ways, or you can open an existing presentation.

Using the AutoContent Wizard

Suppose you are the director of a travel agency called Gulliver's Travel Incorporated. You have been asked to pitch a new tour line to management, and you want to create a presentation that will not only explain the various tours but also get people excited about the new line. You are trying out PowerPoint for the first time, and you want to take advantage of all the help you can get. For your first presentation, you're going to let the AutoContent Wizard be your guide. The AutoContent Wizard asks a few questions to get the ball rolling and then allows you to select one of its ready-made presentations as a starting point. Once you have selected a presentation type, you can customize the presentation by adding, subtracting, or changing various elements. Follow the steps on the next page to use the AutoContent Wizard.

New AutoContent presentations

To use the AutoContent Wizard when you are already in PowerPoint, choose New from the file menu, click the Presentations tab, and then double-click the Auto-Content Wizard icon.

1. With the PowerPoint dialog box open on your screen, be sure the AutoContent Wizard option is selected (if it isn't, click it), and then click OK to display the first of four AutoContent Wizard dialog boxes. (If the Office Assistant reappears, click the second option to turn it off.)

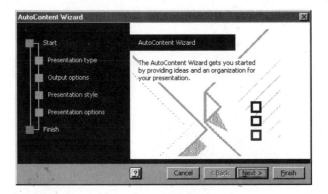

Wizards

Wizards are tools that are incorporated into several Microsoft applications to help you accomplish specific tasks. They work in the same basic way, regardless of the task or the application. Wizards consist of a series of dialog boxes that ask you to provide information or to select from various options. You move from box to box by clicking the Next button, and you can move back to an earlier box by clicking the Back button. Clicking Cancel aborts the entire procedure. Clicking Finish tells the wizard to complete the task with the current settings. Some wizards, like the AutoContent Wizard, include a "road map" with colored boxes representing the wizard's steps. You can see where you are in the process by glancing at the boxes, and you can jump to a particular step by clicking its box.

2. Read the information in the dialog box, and then click Next to move to this dialog box, where you select the type of presentation you want to create:

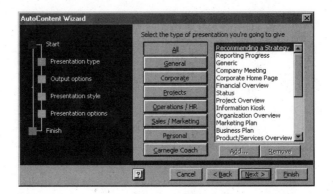

The "road map" on the left tells you to specify a presentation type. All the types are listed on the right, and the buttons in the middle allow you to display the types by category.

3. Click the buttons in the middle of the dialog box to see the presentation types in each category. When you're ready, click the Sales/Marketing button, and with Marketing Plan selected, click Next to display this dialog box:

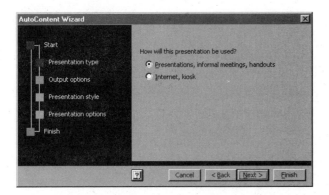

4. Click Next to accept the default option (the first option) for how the presentation will be used and to display the dialog box shown here:

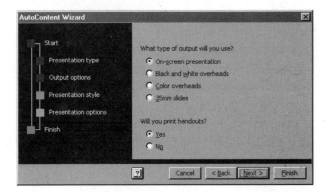

5. Check that On-Screen Presentation is selected as your output option and that Yes is selected in the Will You Print Handouts section, and then click Next to display this dialog box:

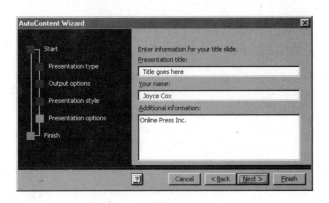

Adding and removing presentation types

If you use only a few presentation types but they are scattered across several categories, you can list them all in one category for convenience. Click that category's button and then click the Add button in the second AutoContent Wizard dialog box. In the Select Presentation Template dialog box, select the presentation type and click Open. To remove a presentation type from a category, select it and click Remove. PowerPoint warns you that if the type is no longer listed in at least one category, removing it will make it inaccessible via the Auto-Content Wizard.

The title slide

The information you enter in this dialog box will become the first slide, called the *title slide*, of the presentation. In the last two edit boxes, PowerPoint may have entered the name and company name used when the program was installed.

6. Replace the text in the top edit box with *Paranormal Tours*, then replace the name in the middle edit box with *Lilly Peushin*, and change the company name in the bottom edit box to *Gulliver's Travel Incorporated*. Click Next to display the AutoContent Wizard's final dialog box, shown here:

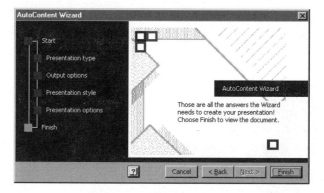

7. Click Finish. PowerPoint opens a presentation window like this one:

Color slide miniature

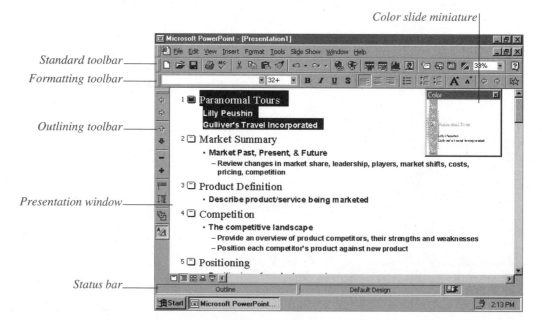

Standard toolbar

Formatting toolbar

Outlining toolbar

Presentation window

Status bar

Like most Windows applications, the Microsoft PowerPoint window includes a title bar, a menu bar, toolbars, and a status bar. Let's pause to take a quick look at each of them.

The Microsoft PowerPoint *title bar* identifies the program. At its left end is the Control menu icon (the miniature slide next to the words *Microsoft PowerPoint*), which provides commands for manipulating the application's window.

The Control menu

The *menu bar* changes to reflect the menus and commands available for the presentation component we are working with. To choose a command from a menu, first click the name of the menu in the menu bar. When the menu drops down, click the name of the desired command. To close a menu without choosing a command, click anywhere outside the menu or press the Esc key.

Choosing commands

On the menus, some command names are displayed in gray letters, indicating that we can't choose those commands at this time, and some command names have an arrowhead next to them, indicating that choosing the command will display a *submenu*. We choose a submenu command the same way we choose a regular command.

Submenus

Some command names are followed by an ellipsis (...), indicating that we must supply more information in a *dialog box* before PowerPoint can carry out the command. We sometimes give the necessary information by typing in an edit box. At other times, we might select options from list boxes or from groups of check boxes and option buttons. We'll use many types of dialog boxes as we progress through this book, and you'll see how easy they are to work with.

The *toolbars* are rows of buttons that quickly access the most commonly used menu commands. Currently, we see the Standard and Formatting toolbars across the top of the window and the Outlining toolbar down the left side. (You may also see a "floating" Common Tasks toolbar.) To avoid confusion, a feature called *ToolTips* helps us determine the functions of each button. When we point to a button, ToolTips displays a pop-up box with the button's name.

Object menus

For efficiency, the commands you are likely to use with a particular element of a presentation (such as a bulleted list) or the presentation window (such as a toolbar) are grouped on special menus called *object menus*. You can display an element's object menu by pointing to the element and clicking the right mouse button. (This action is known as *right-clicking*.) In this book, we give instructions for choosing object menu commands when that is the most efficient way of accomplishing a task.

The *status bar* at the bottom of the window displays messages and gives helpful information.

Outline view →

Taking up most of the screen is our new presentation, which PowerPoint displays in *outline view* in the presentation window. The first topic is the title-slide information we entered in the fifth AutoContent Wizard dialog box. The remaining topics are PowerPoint's suggestions for items we might want to cover in a marketing plan. Each topic is designated by a number and a small slide icon to indicate that the topic will appear as the title of a slide. Subtopics are indented and bulleted to indicate that they will appear as bulleted items on their respective slides.

The slide miniature →

PowerPoint also displays a *Color slide miniature* so that you can see the default design template assigned to this presentation. (We talk more about templates on page 35.)

Saving a Presentation

Before we go any further, let's save the presentation. To save a new presentation, click the Save button or choose Save As from the File menu. PowerPoint then displays a dialog box in which we specify the presentation's name. (Thereafter, clicking the Save button or choosing the Save command will save the presentation without displaying the Save As dialog box, because the presentation already has a name.) Here we go:

1. Choose Save As from the File menu. PowerPoint displays the Save As dialog box:

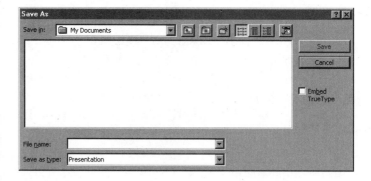

More about toolbars

Some toolbars appear "docked" at the top, bottom, or sides of the window, while others "float" somewhere over the window. To convert a docked toolbar to a floating toolbar, double-click the left end of a horizontal toolbar or the top of a vertical one. Double-click the title bar of a floating toolbar to dock it. You can move a floating toolbar to a new position by dragging its title bar. If you drag to the top, bottom, or sides of the screen, the toolbar arranges itself along that edge of the presentation window. To return a toolbar to its original location, simply drag it back to that spot. You can customize toolbars by moving, removing, and adding toolbar buttons. For more information, check the toolbars topics in PowerPoint's online help index. (We discuss the help feature on page 28.)

2. With the insertion point in the File Name edit box, type *Paranormal Tours*.

3. Be sure the My Documents folder appears in the Save In box and, leaving the other settings in the dialog box as they are, click Save. When you return to the presentation, notice that Paranormal Tours has replaced Presentation1 in the title bar.

From now on, we can simply click the Save button any time we want to save changes to this presentation. Because Power-Point knows the name of the presentation, it overwrites the previous version with the new version. If we want to save our changes but preserve the previous version, we can assign a different name to the new version by choosing the Save As command from the File menu, entering the new name in the File Name edit box, and clicking Save.

The Save button

Saving with a new name

Switching Views

Above the status bar in the bottom left corner of the presentation window is a row of buttons we can use to switch from one view of a presentation to another. Right now, we are in outline view, where we can see all the topics and bulleted lists of a presentation in outline form. We can enter and edit text in this view, but as we discuss on page 48, we'll probably use outline view mainly for reorganizing the topics and bulleted items of our slides. We introduce the other views as we work through this book.

Let's move to *slide view*, where we can concentrate on the content of the presentation one slide at a time. Follow the steps on the next page to switch to slide view.

Slide view

Saving options

A presentation will be saved in the folder designated in the Save In box. If you want to store a presentation in a different folder, click the arrow to the right of the Save In box and navigate to that folder before clicking Save. If the folder you want doesn't exist, you can create the folder by clicking the Create New Folder button and naming the folder before you save the file. To save a presentation in a format other than that of a normal PowerPoint presentation, select the format you want from the Save As Type drop-down list before clicking Save. For example, you can save a presentation in a previous version of PowerPoint, but you may lose some of its formatting.

The Slide View button

1. Click the Slide View button in the bottom left corner of the presentation window, or choose Slide from the View menu.

2. If necessary, close the Common Tasks toolbar by clicking its Close button (the X). Your screen now looks like this:

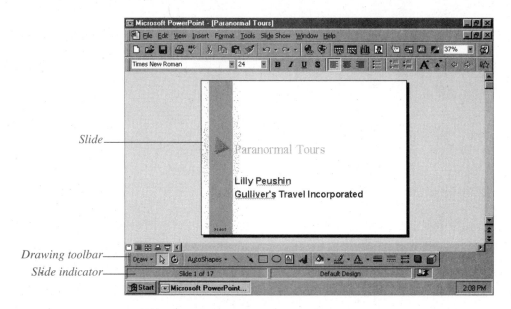

Slide

Drawing toolbar

Slide indicator

PowerPoint displays the title slide of the presentation with the formatting of the design template assigned to this presentation type. (See page 35 for more about templates.) The red, wavy underlines beneath the words *Peushin* and *Gulliver's* indicate that these words are not in PowerPoint's spelling dictionary and may be misspellings. (We discuss spell-checking on page 43.) Notice that the right scroll bar now has Previous Slide and Next Slide buttons, which we can click to move backward and forward through the presentation's slides.

The Previous Slide and Next Slide buttons

Editing Slides

Now we're ready to customize the text of the slides created by the AutoContent Wizard. We can work with text in both slide and outline views. In a strong presentation, each slide must stand on its own as well as contribute to the overall message, so when we first start creating presentations, we will probably want to work in slide view to see how each slide looks. Once we have a few presentations under our belt, we might find it quicker to work in outline view and then switch to slide view to see the results. In either case, we can go back and make changes at any time, so don't worry about getting stuck with something less than perfect. In fact, it's often best to leave the fine-tuning until the end of the development process; too much fussing can bog down even a short project.

Editing Bulleted and Subordinate Items

Let's edit the existing slides so that they provide details about the new Paranormal Tours line. Follow these steps:

1. Click the Next Slide button at the bottom of the right scroll bar to move to the second slide, which looks like this:

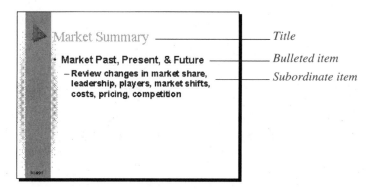

This slide has a *title* (its topic), a *bulleted item*, and a *subordinate item*.

2. Using any standard Windows selection technique, select the title text and type *Objectives*. (Notice that PowerPoint surrounds the *title area* with a shaded border.)

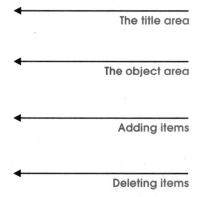

The title area

3. Next select the text of the bulleted item (a shaded border appears around the *object area*) and type the following:

   To provide new tour packages for affiliated agencies

The object area

4. Press Enter to create a second bulleted item and type:

   To satisfy the public's increasing interest in the paranormal

Adding items

5. Select the text of the subordinate item and press Delete or Backspace to delete it. (The bullet disappears when you click elsewhere on the slide.) The results are shown on the next page.

Deleting items

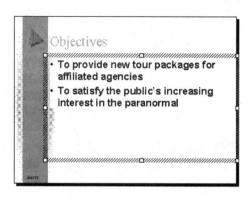

6. Save your changes. (Remember to save at regular intervals as you work. A good rule of thumb is to save anything you don't want to do over again.)

Slide 2 looks pretty good, so let's move on:

1. Click the Next Slide button to display Slide 3.

2. Replace the title text with *Customer Requirements*.

3. Next, replace the text of the bulleted item with *Tours that are not only insightful but enjoyable* (without a period).

4. Press Enter to create a second bulleted item and type *Tours that focus on the latest developments in paranormalism*.

5. Press Enter to create a third bulleted item and type *Tour packages that are flexible*. Here are the results:

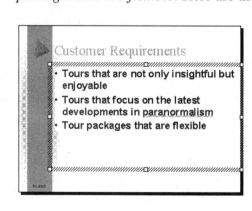

Undoing and redoing multiple actions

If you make a mistake while creating a presentation, you can click the Undo button on the Standard toolbar to reverse your last action. To reinstate that action, click the Redo button on the Standard toolbar. You can also undo and redo multiple actions at a time. Click the arrow to the right of the appropriate button and drag through the actions in the list that you want to undo or redo. You can't undo or redo a single action other than the last one (which is the first one in the list). For example, to undo the third action in the list, you must also undo the first and the second. To change the number of actions you want PowerPoint to track in the Undo/Redo lists, choose Options from the Tools menu, click the Edit tab, and change the number in the Maximum Number Of Undos box.

Promoting and Demoting Items

On page 13, we deleted a subordinate item from Slide 2. But sometimes we will need to add subordinate items in order to get our point across. And sometimes we will need to convert a bulleted item to a subordinate item, and vice versa. Let's experiment a bit:

1. Click the Next Slide button to move to Slide 4, and change the title to *Some Sample Tours*.

2. Replace the text of the first bulleted item with *Ghostly Bed & Breakfasts*.

3. Next, replace the text of the first subordinate item with *United States*.

4. Now you want to convert the second subordinate item into a main bulleted item. Click an insertion point in the second subordinate item and then click the Promote button on the Formatting toolbar. PowerPoint changes the bullet character and moves the line out to the margin.

The Promote button

5. Replace the text of this item with *Mythical Monsters*.

6. Press Enter and type *Extraterrestrial Exploration*.

7. Now suppose you want to add a subordinate item after the first bulleted item. Click an insertion point to the right of the *s* in *Breakfasts* and press Enter to create a new bulleted item. Then click the Demote button on the Formatting toolbar. PowerPoint changes the bullet character and indents the line

The Demote button

Selecting parts of a slide

You can use many of the standard Windows text-selection techniques when editing text in both slide and outline views. For example, you can double-click a word to select it. In slide view, you can select an entire text object, such as a bulleted list, by clicking the object and then either choosing Select All from the Edit menu or pressing Ctrl+A. In outline view, you can click a bullet to select the bulleted item and its subordinate items. Also in outline view, you can click the slide icon to the left of a topic to select the topic and all of its bulleted items.

Five levels of bullets

With PowerPoint, you can create up to five levels of bulleted items on a slide, but we recommend that you use no more than two. Using more than two levels almost always results in crowded slides that are difficult to read and hard to understand.

to show that this item is subordinate to the preceding one. Type *Europe*. Slide 4 now looks like this:

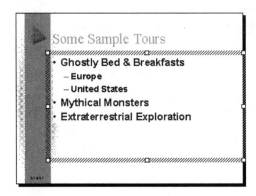

Let's quickly edit the text of the remaining slides of the Paranormal Tours presentation. Along the way, you'll notice misspelled words in bold. Be sure to type the words exactly as they appear so that you have something to correct when we check spelling in Chapter 2. Follow these steps:

1. Click the Next Slide button to display Slide 5.

2. Replace the title with *Customer **Sirvey*** and replace the first bulleted item with *Over the last **dekade**, public interest in paranormal phenomena has increased 40%.*

3. Select the remaining text on the slide and press Delete. Slide 5 now looks like this:

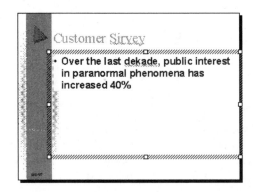

4. Click the Next Slide button and type *Typical **Toor** Package Prices* as Slide 6's title. Then delete the two bulleted items. PowerPoint won't delete the first bullet character until you add another object, such as a graph or table, to the object area; however, when the slide is displayed in slide show view or printed, the bullet will not be visible. In Chapter 3, we'll add a table to this slide's object area.

5. Click the Next Slide button, and change the title to *Affiliated Agencies*. Then select all of the bulleted text and press Delete. We'll add an organizational chart to this slide in Chapter 3.

6. Click the Next Slide button to display Slide 8, which will be the final slide in the Paranormal Tours presentation.

7. Replace the title with *Wrap Up* and replace the first bulleted item with *By endorsing the Paranormal Tours line, Gulliver's Travel Incorporated will be at the forefront of worldwide travel agencies*. Delete the remaining text on the slide. Here's what the slide looks like:

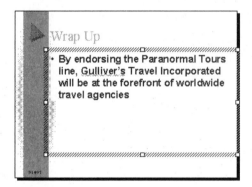

Deleting Slides

We've completed the "first draft" of the Paranormal Tours presentation, but we still need to get rid of the extraneous slides created by the AutoContent Wizard. Deleting slides is easy to accomplish in outline view, so let's switch to that view now and delete the last nine slides of the presentation. Follow the steps on the next page.

The fewer bulleted items the better

With the current design template, you can enter eight single-line bulleted items in the object area, but eight is really too many. The more bullets on a slide, the harder it is for your audience to focus on any one of the points you are trying to make. You have a better chance of getting your message across to your audience if you limit the number of bulleted items to six lines. If you have many bulleted items, break them into logical groups and use a different slide for each group.

The Outline View button

Selecting multiple slides

1. Click the Outline View button in the bottom left corner of the window or choose Outline from the View menu. Your screen looks similar to the one shown earlier on page 8, except that the active slide, Slide 8, is selected.

2. Click the slide icon to the left of the topic for Slide 9 to select it, scroll the window so that you can see Slide 17, hold down the Shift key, and click the slide icon for Slide 17. The last nine slides in the presentation are now selected.

3. Press Delete to delete the selected slides, and then press Ctrl+Home to move to the beginning of the presentation.

4. Click the Save button to safeguard your work.

Now that we have a workable set of slides, let's see how we might use them to give a presentation to others.

Delivering a Presentation

When we created the Paranormal Tours presentation, the AutoContent Wizard presented us with the following output options: On-Screen Presentation, Black And White Overheads, Color Overheads, and 35mm Slides. Depending on such factors as the presentation type and the size of our audience, we might need to use any of these options, so we cover them all in this section.

Running an Electronic Slide Show

Electronic slide shows

On-screen presentations, also known as *electronic slide shows*, are gaining in popularity, partly because being able to deliver an electronic slide show conveys an impression of being "up" on the latest technology, and partly because electronic slide shows allow us to interact with the presentation in ways that are not possible with static overheads and 35mm slides. Because the slide show is delivered from the computer, it can incorporate special effects, such as the wipes and fades associated with video and television productions (see page 136), and it can skip slides or branch off in new directions as appropriate (see page 144). An electronic slide show can even incorporate audio, video, and animation segments developed with other programs, and it can be set to run automatically, either at a predefined pace that keeps in sync with a presenter or independently, as a stand-alone presentation (see page 133).

We'll talk more about equipment needs and the logistics of preparing for an electronic slide show in Chapter 6. For now, let's simply see how to view a slide show on your computer. There are two ways to deliver an electronic slide show: with PowerPoint and with PowerPoint Viewer. We discuss Power-Point Viewer on page 153. Here, we'll cover how to run Paranormal Tours as an electronic slide show from Power-Point itself. Let's experiment:

1. With the insertion point located in Slide 1 of Paranormal Tours, click the Slide Show button in the bottom left corner of the window to display the first slide of the presentation in slide show view, like this:

The Slide Show button

2. To move to the next slide, click the left mouse button or press the PageDown key.

3. Continue clicking the left mouse button to step through the slides one at a time. (To move to the previous slide, simply click the right mouse button and choose Previous from the object menu, or press the PageUp key. You can cancel the slide show at any time by pressing Esc.)

Starting slide shows from Explorer

You can start a slide show automatically by right-clicking a presentation in Windows Explorer and choosing Show from the object menu.

When we click the left mouse button with the last slide displayed, PowerPoint switches back to the view we were in before we clicked the Slide Show button. We show you how to avoid this rather abrupt return to reality in Chapter 6 (see page 134). We also show you how to add all sorts of special effects. In the meantime, you now know how to create and run simple electronic slide shows from your computer. In the next sections, we'll look at how to prepare presentations for output in two familiar formats: overhead transparencies and 35mm slides.

Printing Overheads

In spite of all the advances in presentation technology, black-and-white or color overhead transparencies are still the medium of choice for the majority of people. Although the price of display equipment is tumbling, the fact is that most people don't want or need to purchase special equipment for the rare occasion when they are called upon to make a presentation. If making presentations is part of your job or if your future career hinges on the impact of a particular presentation, you will probably discount overheads in favor of 35mm slides or an electronic slide show. But be warned: no amount of high-tech gadgetry can make up for a mediocre delivery style. When all is said and done, it is what you say—not what you show your audience—that will win them over.

In the next example, we give instructions for printing black-and-white overheads, but the steps for printing color overheads are essentially the same. If you have a color printer at your disposal, feel free to print color overheads instead. Here are the steps:

Slide show tools

When you move the mouse pointer across a slide in slide show view, a button appears in the bottom left corner of the screen. You can click the button to display a menu of helpful slide show tools. (We discuss these tools on page 132.)

1. Turn on your printer and load the paper tray with at least four sheets of acetate.

2. To avoid confusion about what you are printing, switch to slide view and display Slide 1 of Paranormal Tours.

3. Next, choose Page Setup from the File menu to display this dialog box:

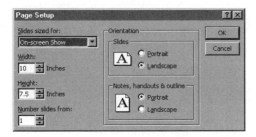

4. Click the arrow to the right of the Slides Sized For box, select Overhead from the drop-down list, and then click OK. Now the slide images will fill the acetate pages.

5. Choose Print from the File menu to display this dialog box:

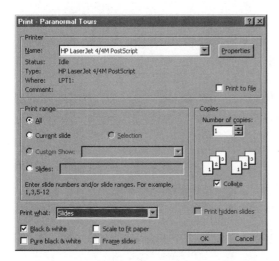

To print the entire presentation with the default settings in this dialog box, you can click the Print button on the Standard

The Print button

Printer setup

If your computer can access more than one printer or if you need to set up the printer to print with PowerPoint, click the arrow to the right of the Name box in the Print dialog box and select the printer from the drop-down list. Then make any necessary adjustments by clicking the Properties button to access the printer's Properties dialog box. For example, you can switch between portrait and landscape printing on the Page tab.

toolbar. To print only the active slide or only specific slides, or to change any of the options at the bottom of the Print dialog box, you must choose the Print command.

6. Be sure the Black & White option is selected and click OK. (If you're printing color overheads, deselect the Black & White option and click OK.) PowerPoint prints an overhead for each of the slides shown at the beginning of the chapter.

Now all you need is an overhead projector and an audience, and you're ready to give your first presentation.

Preparing a File for Slides

The simplest way to output a presentation as a set of 35mm slides is to entrust the imaging procedure to Genigraphics, a service bureau located in Memphis, TN. We prepare the presentation file for outputting as slides by "printing" the file using the Genigraphics software that is shipped with Power-Point. A communications program called GraphicsLink is also included so that if we have a modem, we can simply send the presentation file to Genigraphics electronically. Other-wise, we can send the file on disk. Before we get started, take a moment to determine whether the Genigraphics software has been installed on your computer by checking the File menu. If the Genigraphics command is not available on the Send To submenu, follow the instructions in the adjacent tip to install the Genigraphics and GraphicsLink programs. If the Genigraphics command is available, follow these steps:

1. With Slide 1 of the Paranormal Tours presentation displayed on your screen, choose Page Setup from the File menu to display the dialog box shown on the previous page. Click the arrow to the right of the Slides Sized For box, select 35mm Slides from the drop-down list, and then click OK.

2. Next choose Send To and then Genigraphics from the File menu to start the Genigraphics Wizard and display the dialog box shown at the top of the facing page.

Installing the Genigraphics programs

To install the Genigraphics soft-ware, choose Settings and then Control Panel from the Windows 95 Start menu, and then double-click the Add/Remove Programs icon. Select Microsoft Office 97 or Microsoft PowerPoint 97 and click the Add/Remove button. When prompted, insert the ap-propriate disk, and then follow the instructions on the screen, changing the PowerPoint options to include Genigraphics Wizard & GraphicsLink.

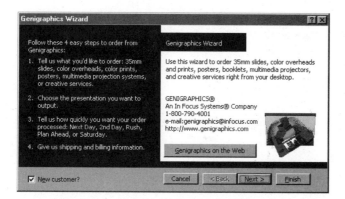

3. Read the information in the dialog box and click Next to display the wizard's second dialog box:

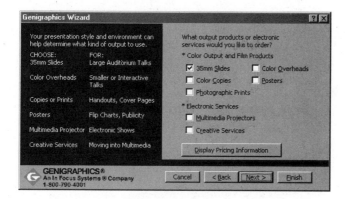

4. Be sure the 35mm Slides option is selected and then click Next to display this dialog box:

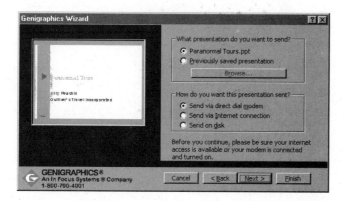

Other available output options

In addition to 35mm slides, service bureaus (such as Genigraphics) can output several other presentation media. Options include color overheads, copies or photographic prints, and posters. These service bureaus can also help with other electronic multimedia services.

5. Paranormal Tours should be selected in the What Presentation Do You Want To Send section. If it isn't, select it. If you don't

see Paranormal Tours in this section, select the Previously Saved Presentation option, click the Browse button, and then locate and select the Paranormal Tours presentation.

6. Depending on whether you have a modem, select the appropriate option in the How Do You Want This Presentation Sent section and then click Next to display the wizard's fourth dialog box:

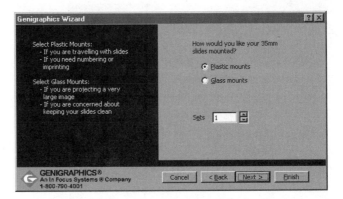

7. Select the mounting option (Plastic Mounts is the default), specify the number of slide sets you want, and click Next. The wizard displays its fifth dialog box:

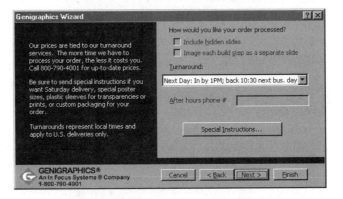

8. Click the arrow to the right of the Turnaround box to see the various turnaround options Genigraphics offers. If you want, select a different option and then click Next. (You can also include special instructions by clicking the Special Instructions button and typing them in the dialog box that appears.)

9. In the wizard's sixth dialog box, select an option in the Delivery Charges section and fill in the appropriate shipping information. Click Next to display this dialog box:

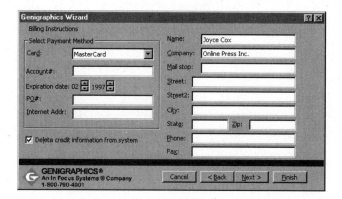

10. Fill in your credit card and billing information and click Next. In the wizard's final dialog box, check that the shipping and billing information is correct and then check the information in the instructions box on the right. (If you need to make a change, click the Back button until the appropriate dialog box is displayed and then make your change.) When you're ready, click Finish.

11. If you plan to mail a disk to Genigraphics, you'll see the Save As dialog box. Click the Save button to save the presentation and your instructions as a Genigraphics file. You can then copy the file to a disk and send it to the address given in the wizard's final dialog box. If you plan to send your presentation file via modem, you'll see the GraphicsLink dialog box, which reports on the status of the transmission.

With the help of Genigraphics, creating 35mm slides for a presentation is fairly painless. Keep in mind, however, that we're not restricted to this service bureau. We can send a presentation file that has been formatted for 35mm slides to any company that provides this type of service.

Creating Speaker's Notes

With any presentation, we are probably going to want to jot down a few notes to remind ourselves of the points we want to make while displaying each slide. (With an electronic slide show, we will also want to include instructions about marking up slides, displaying hidden slides, or branching to subordinate presentations. See Chapter 6 for more information.) In PowerPoint, we can generate a notes page for each slide, complete with a thumbnail sketch of the slide itself and any additional information we want to add. Let's create notes pages for the slides in Paranormal Tours:

The Notes Page View button

1. With Slide 1 of the Paranormal Tours presentation displayed in slide view, click the Notes Page View button in the bottom left corner of the window. PowerPoint displays this notes page for the first slide:

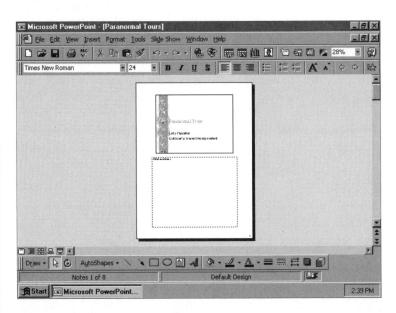

Adding notes while creating a presentation

If you prefer to write speaker's notes as you create and edit your presentation, choose Speaker Notes from the View menu. PowerPoint displays a Speaker Notes dialog box where you can type notes about the current slide. If you want to write notes about more than one slide at a time, leave the Speaker Notes dialog box open, select another slide, and type the notes. PowerPoint attaches the notes to the selected slide. When you finish adding notes, click the Close button to close the dialog box.

2. Click the arrow to the right of the Zoom box on the Standard toolbar and select 100% from the drop-down list to zoom in on the notes area of the page.

3. Click the notes area, type *Site recent trends showing an increased interest in all things paranormal*, press Enter, and

type *Remind about our reputation for innovation.* Then make up two or three more notes.

4. It's a good idea to make the important words on the notes page stand out so that you can simply glance at the page rather than having to read it. Select *trends* in the first note and click the Bold button, and then repeat this step with *reputation for innovation* in the second note and key words in any remaining notes.

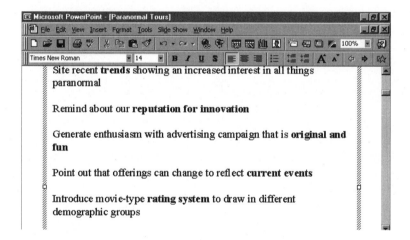

The Bold button

5. Select all the notes and change the font size by clicking the arrow to the right of the Font Size box on the Formatting toolbar and selecting 14 or 16. (You can also choose the Line Spacing command from the Format menu to change the space between the notes.) Here are the results:

6. Click the Save button to save the new notes page.

When you're ready, follow the steps below to print the speaker's notes:

1. Choose Print from the File menu to display the Print dialog box (see page 21).

Printing speaker's notes

2. Click the arrow to the right of the Print What box and select Notes Pages from the drop-down list.

3. Make any necessary changes to the other settings in the dialog box and click OK. Then click the Slide View button to return to slide view.

PowerPoint prints the notes pages in portrait (vertical) mode. If you want to change the orientation to landscape (horizontal) mode, choose Page Setup from the File menu and select the Landscape option in the Notes, Handouts & Outline section of the Page Setup dialog box.

Printing Handouts

If we want to provide handouts so that our audience has a paper copy of the material we are presenting, we can print as many as six slides per sheet of paper. Let's print handouts for the Paranormal Tours presentation:

1. With Slide 1 displayed on your screen, choose Print from the File menu.

2. When the Print dialog box appears, click the arrow to the right of the Print What box and select the Handouts (2 Slides Per Page) option.

3. Click OK to print four handout pages.

Well, that wraps up our discussion of the various ways you can give a presentation using PowerPoint. Before we end the chapter, though, we'll take a quick look at how to get help if you get stuck.

Getting Help

This tour of PowerPoint has covered a lot of ground in just a few pages, and you might be wondering how you will manage to retain it all. Don't worry. If we forget how to carry out a particular task, help is never far away. We've already seen how the ToolTips feature can jog our memory about the functions of the toolbar buttons. And you may have noticed that the dialog boxes contain a Help button (the question mark) you can click to get information about their options. Here, we'll look at ways to get information using the Office Assistant, a new feature of PowerPoint 97, which you've probably seen pop up a few times already. Follow these steps:

Creating handouts in Word

If you have Microsoft Word installed on your computer, you have more options for producing notes and handouts for your presentations. Switch to black and white view by clicking the Black And White View button on the Standard toolbar. Then choose Send To and Microsoft Word from the File menu. PowerPoint displays the Write-Up dialog box, where you can select from several layout options, as well as an Outline Only option. Select the option that suits your needs, select either Paste or Paste Link at the bottom of the dialog box, and click OK. Word then opens and creates the notes or handouts in the layout you selected. If you selected Paste, the slides are embedded as-is in the Word document. If you selected Paste Link, however, the document's slide images are linked to the presentation's slides and will be updated to reflect any changes you make to the presentation.

1. Click the Office Assistant button on the Standard toolbar. The ◄───  The Office Assistant button
   Office Assistant appears, giving you several options for pro-
   ceeding, as shown here:

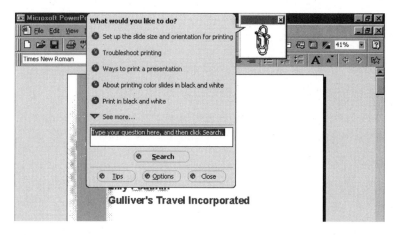

2. The Office Assistant's options reflect the work you have been
   doing. If you don't find any of the current options helpful,
   you can type a question in the Search box and then click the
   Search button to have the Office Assistant search for topics
   that most closely match your question.

3. Type *How do I make handouts?* and click the Search button.
   The Office Assistant then displays a list of topics related to
   your question.

4. Click the Create Speaker Notes And Handouts option to
   display the Help window shown below. (It may take a few
   seconds while the Help file is being prepared.)

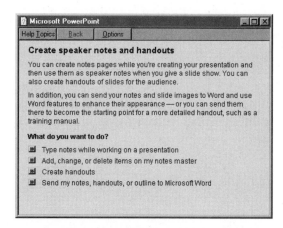

5. Read through the information and then click the arrow next to the Create Handouts option to display instructions on how to complete the task.

6. Click the Back button to move back to the Create Speaker Notes And Handouts topic, and explore other options.

7. Click the Help window's Close button and then click the Office Assistant's Close button.

If you prefer to get help without the aid of the Office Assistant, you can use the Help menu. Follow these steps:

1. Choose Contents And Index from the Help menu and, if necessary, click the Index tab to display this dialog box:

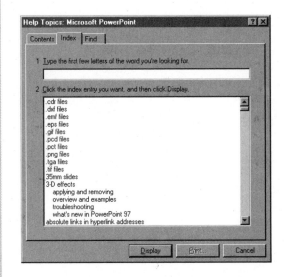

2. In the edit box, type *hand*. The list below scrolls to display topics beginning with the letters you type.

3. With Handouts highlighted in the list of index entries, click the Display button. Then select Create Speaker Notes And Handouts in the Topics Found window and click Display again. Help displays the information shown on page 29. Click the Close button.

We'll leave you to explore other Help topics on your own.

Quitting PowerPoint

You have seen how to use PowerPoint to create a simple text-based presentation. Easy, wasn't it? All that's left is to show you how to end a PowerPoint session. Follow these steps:

1. Choose Exit from the File menu.

2. If PowerPoint asks whether you want to save the changes you have made to the open presentation, click Yes.

Here are some other ways to quit PowerPoint:

- Click the Close button at the right end of PowerPoint's title bar.

- Press Alt, then F (the underlined letter in *File* on the menu bar), then X (the underlined letter in *Exit* on the File menu).

- Double-click the Control menu icon—the small slide next to the words *Microsoft PowerPoint*—at the left end of Power-Point's title bar.

Using the Web for help

If you have a modem and are connected to the Internet, you can quickly access Microsoft's Web site to get help or technical support. Simply choose Microsoft On The Web from the Help menu to display a submenu, and then choose the appropriate option.

Fine-Tuning a Presentation 2

We create a second presentation using a design template adding slides and switching templates along the way. Then we format, edit, and spell-check the text of the slides. Finally, we rearrange the slides of the presentation using outline and slide sorter views.

We created a presentation based on a design template and added formatting to individual slides. Then we spell-checked and edited an existing presentation, reorganizing text and entire slides.

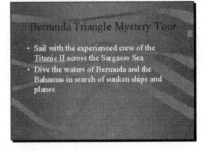

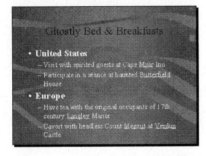

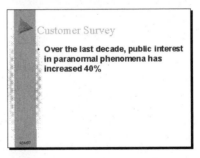

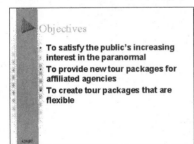

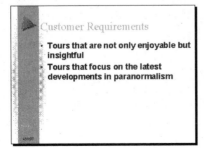

In Chapter 1, we created a presentation using one of the AutoContent Wizard's ready-made presentation types and then tailored the text of its topics, bulleted items, and subordinate items to meet our needs. In this chapter, we create a new presentation based on a design template, adding slides and text as we go along. Then we show you various ways of fine-tuning a presentation by editing and formatting text and rearranging slides to strengthen your argument.

Before we get going, we want to remind you of the characteristics that distinguish a good presentation from a bad one. PowerPoint, for all its fancy features, is just a tool. The overall effectiveness of our presentation depends on our thoughtful planning and attention to the smallest details. It is easy to mar a presentation produced in PowerPoint with bad characteristics such as small fonts, extraneous details, and distracting visual embellishments. Here are some pointers for creating clear, concise slides:

The audience → • Put yourself in the shoes of your audience. You should know as much as possible about them before you start creating your presentation, and tailor its tone, words, and graphics appropriately.

The overall theme → • What points do you want your audience to remember one hour after your presentation? One week? You can facilitate their recall by coming up with an overall theme that you can reinforce throughout the presentation.

One main idea → • Make each slide responsible for conveying only one main idea that can be interpreted at a glance.

No extra words → • Cut the verbiage on each slide to the essentials. Never have more than six bulleted items on a slide. The more bulleted items you have, the fewer words you should use in each item.

Consistency → • Make sure your capitalization and punctuation is consistent throughout your presentation and that your slide titles are constructed in similar ways. On any one slide, don't mix complete sentences and partial sentences.

As we said before, don't expect your slides to carry the entire weight of the presentation. When it comes right down to it, *you* are giving the presentation, not your visual aids. To hold the attention of your audience—large or small—you must be poised and confident, and you must express your ideas clearly and persuasively. Many day-to-day business activities—introducing a new product to a customer, conducting a meeting, or negotiating a contract, for example—involve making presentations of one sort or another, with or without visual aids. The ability to speak in front of a group of people is a necessary business skill that is worth cultivating, even if you don't anticipate ever addressing a room full of people.

◄——— Speaking skills

Using a Design Template

If we know exactly what we want to say but we need a little help coming up with a design for our presentation, we can bypass the AutoContent Wizard and start a presentation based on one of PowerPoint's design templates. A *template* is a set of ready-made formatting that defines the look of a slide. PowerPoint comes with many templates that incorporate different combinations of graphic, typographic, and special effects. Often one of these templates is just what we need to give a presentation an appropriate, professional look. And, if we later change our mind about the design we have chosen, we can easily switch to a different template with just a few mouse clicks.

◄——— Templates

Follow the steps below to create a presentation using a design template:

1. Start PowerPoint by choosing Programs and then Microsoft PowerPoint from the Start menu.

2. When the PowerPoint dialog box appears, double-click the Template option to open the New Presentation dialog box, and then, if necessary, click the Presentation Designs tab to display the template options shown on the next page.

Black and white view

To see how a presentation looks in black and white, click the Black And White View button on the Standard toolbar. A Color slide miniature shows the underlying color design. (If this slide miniature does not appear automatically, choose Slide Miniature from the View menu to turn it on. You can also display a Black And White slide miniature by choosing Slide Miniature from the View menu while in color view.) Click the Black And White View button again to return to color view and to close the Color slide miniature.

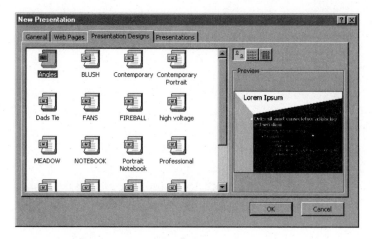

Previewing templates

3. Click any template icon and check the Preview box on the right to see a sample of the template. Click other template icons, noticing their different designs.

4. When you're ready, double-click the Pulse icon. PowerPoint opens the New Slide dialog box shown below:

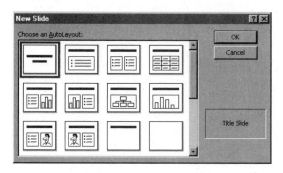

Autolayouts

PowerPoint provides 23 predefined slide layouts, called *auto-layouts*, plus one blank slide that you can use to design a slide layout of your own. You can scroll the other autolayouts into view by using the scroll bar on the right.

5. Click the second autolayout in the top row and click OK to create a bulleted list slide.

6. Save the presentation with the name *Sample Tours*.

Slide 1 is now ready and awaiting our input:

1. Click the title area and type *Extraterrestrial Exploration*.

2. Click the object area and type *Visit top-secret Area 51 in Nevada* as the first bulleted item.

3. Press Enter to start another bulleted item and then type *Search for UFO wreckage in Roswell, New Mexico.*

4. Press Enter again and type *Tour the set of the hit movie Aliens Among Us.* The results are shown below:

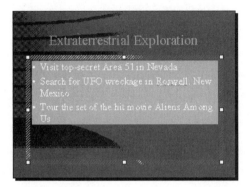

Adding Slides

When we create a presentation based on a design template, PowerPoint provides only the initial slide. If we click the Next Slide button, PowerPoint beeps and nothing happens, because this is the last slide in the presentation. To add three more slides to Sample Tours, follow these steps:

1. With Slide 1 displayed on the screen, click the New Slide button on the Standard toolbar to open the New Slide dialog box.

The New Slide button

2. Be sure the Bulleted List autolayout is selected and click OK to add a second slide to your presentation.

3. Click the title area of Slide 2 and type *Mythical Monsters.*

4. In the object area, type *Roam the Cascade Mountains of the Pacific Northwest in search of Bigfoot* as the first bulleted item. Press Enter and type *Explore the deep waters of Loch Ness* as the second bulleted item. Press Enter a third time and type *Test your climbing skills in the Himalayas, home of the Yeti* as the last bulleted item.

5. Repeat steps 1 and 2 above to add a new bulleted list slide and then type *Ghostly Bed & Breakfasts* as the title.

6. Click the object area of Slide 3 and type these bulleted items, using the Demote button on the Formatting toolbar to create the subordinate items:

- *United States*
    - *Visit with spirited guests at Cape Muir Inn*
    - *Participate in a séance at haunted Butterfield House*
- *Europe*
    - *Have tea with the original occupants of 17th century Langley Manor*
    - *Cavort with headless Count Meeout at Verdun Castle*

7. Add a fourth bulleted list slide and type *Bermuda Triangle Mystery Tour* as the title. Then type these bulleted items:

- *Sail with the experienced crew of the Titanic II across the Sargasso Sea*
- *Dive the waters of Bermuda and the Bahamas in search of sunken ships and planes*

8. Save the Sample Tours presentation.

Switching Templates

After creating the Bermuda Triangle Mystery Tour slide in the Sample Tours presentation, suppose you recall seeing a whirlpool design template in the New Presentation dialog box. Fortunately, PowerPoint makes it easy to switch from one template to another. Here's how:

The Apply Design button

1. With Slide 4 of the Sample Tours presentation displayed on your screen, click the Apply Design button to display the dialog box shown on the facing page.

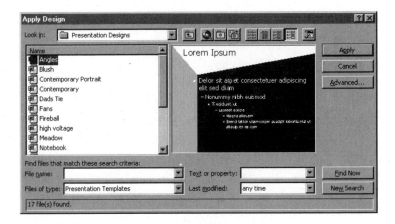

2. Scroll the list and double-click the Whirlpool option. Slide 4 now looks like this:

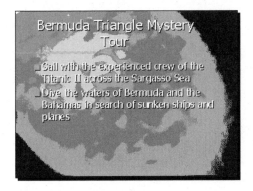

3. Scroll through the other slides in the presentation and note that the Whirlpool template has been applied to them all.

   Although the Whirlpool template is a good choice for Slide 4, it's not appropriate for the other slides in the presentation. Let's check out another design template for Sample Tours:

1. Right-click the background of any displayed slide and choose Apply Design from the object menu.

2. When the Apply Design dialog box appears, double-click the Ribbons option and admire the results.

More templates

If none of the templates provided in the Presentation Designs folder quite fit the bill, you may want to check out the additional templates available in the ValuPack on the Office or PowerPoint installation disk. To view these templates, insert your installation disk, click the Apply Design button, and navigate to the correct disk drive. Then move to the ValuPack Template folder. Here, you can look in the Designs folder for more template designs (many of which are templates that were available in previous versions of PowerPoint) or in the Present folder for additional AutoContent templates.

Formatting Text

We have selected a design template to give our presentation a particular look, but we can still use text formatting to create special effects. For example, we can use the bold style and a larger font size to draw attention to major points and the italic style and a smaller font size to de-emphasize minor points. Let's change some of the text formatting in Sample Tours using buttons on the Formatting toolbar. (In Chapter 5, we'll show you how to format text using the Font command.) Follow these steps:

1. Display Slide 1 and then select *Aliens Among Us* in the last bulleted item.

2. Now take a look at the Formatting toolbar to determine what types of formatting have been applied to the current selection. The Font box at the left end of the toolbar displays *Times New Roman*, which is the current font, and the Font Size box displays 32, which is the current font size. In addition, the Left Alignment and Bullets buttons appear "pressed," indicating that the paragraph containing the current selection is a left-aligned bulleted item.

The Italic button

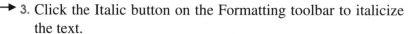

3. Click the Italic button on the Formatting toolbar to italicize the text.

Painting formats

If you want to format a block of text with a set of formats that you have already applied to another block of text, you can copy all the formatting in a simple three-step procedure. Select the text whose formats you want to copy, click the Format Painter button on the Standard toolbar, and then select the text you want to format. PowerPoint duplicates the formatting for the new selection.

Don't go overboard

When you select a font or fonts for your presentation, keep a few simple rules in mind:

● Use one font per slide.
● Use only one or two font styles, such as bold or italic, per slide.
● Watch out for certain style combinations. For example, text that is both italic and outlined is very difficult to read on a monitor or overhead projector.
● Choose fonts that have "clean" shapes. For example, sans serif fonts (those without strokes at the ends of the characters) are easier to read on slides and overhead transparencies than serif fonts.
● If you're having slides or overheads made, be sure your service bureau can output the fonts you select.

4. Now move to Slide 3 and select the text of the first bulleted item, *United States*.

5. Click the arrow to the right of the Font Size box on the Formatting toolbar to display this drop-down list of sizes:

The Font Size box

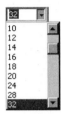

6. Scroll the list and select 36 and then click the Bold button to make the text bold.

7. Select the text of the second bulleted item, *Europe*, and repeat steps 5 and 6 to make the text 36 points and bold.

8. Click anywhere on the slide to deselect the text. Here are the results:

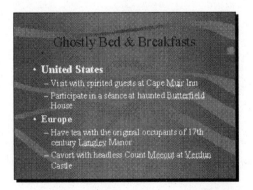

9. Finally, move to Slide 4, select *Titanic II* in the first bulleted item, and then click the Underline button on the Formatting toolbar.

The Underline button

Adding a bit of formatting here and there can certainly improve the look of a presentation. Let's make one more improvement by rebreaking a couple of lines of text on Slide 1:

1. Display Slide 1 and click an insertion point to the left of the *N* in *New* in the second bulleted item.

Rebreaking lines → **2.** Press Shift+Enter to break the line after *Roswell*.

3. In the last bulleted item, click an insertion point to the left of the *A* in *Among* and press Shift+Enter to break the line after *Aliens*. The text of Slide 1 now appears more balanced, as you can see here:

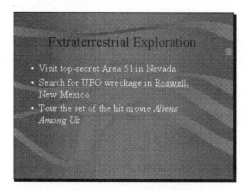

Opening an Existing Presentation

We've pretty much finished with the Sample Tours presentation, and we now want to do some more work on the Paranormal Tours presentation we started in Chapter 1. However, because these two presentations contain some of the same information, we want to keep the Sample Tours presentation close at hand. Let's minimize Sample Tours and open Paranormal Tours:

1. Save Sample Tours and click the presentation window's Minimize button (the minus button at the right end of the menu bar, not PowerPoint's title bar). Sample Tours shrinks

Checking your style

If you are concerned about the spelling, fonts, case, or punctuation of a presentation, you can use the Style Checker to check your work. When you choose Style Checker from the Tools menu, PowerPoint displays a dialog box listing the various elements the Style Checker can review. Included are Spelling, Visual Clarity, and Case And End Punctuation options. (If Visual Clarity is selected, font usage and the legibility of titles and body text are checked.) After making your selections, click the Options button to refine them. For example, you can specify whether titles should have end punctuation, and you can set a minimum font size for body text. When you're ready, click Start in the Style Checker dialog box to begin the review. When the Style Checker is finished, it displays any inconsistencies in the Style Checker Summary dialog box. Make a note of these inconsistencies so that you can correct them if necessary, and then click OK.

until all that is visible is a small title bar in the bottom left corner of the PowerPoint window.

2. Now click the Open button on the Standard toolbar. Power-Point displays this dialog box:

The Open button

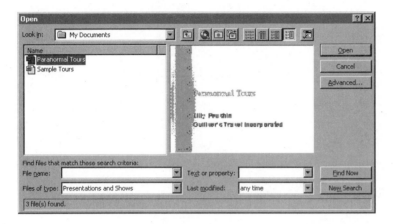

3. Double-click Paranormal Tours in the Name list to open the presentation you created in Chapter 1.

4. If necessary, maximize the window and switch to slide view.

5. Choose Page Setup from the File menu and if necessary, change the Slides Sized For setting to On-Screen Show. Then click OK.

Checking Spelling

As we created the Paranormal Tours presentation, we deliberately included a few errors, and PowerPoint flagged them with red, wavy underlines. This feature, called *automatic spell-checking*, can be turned off by clicking the Hide Spelling Errors check box on the Spelling tab of the Options dialog box. However, leaving automatic spell-checking turned on means we can correct errors as we work. Let's fix one of the misspelled words now:

Automatic spell-checking

1. Use the Next Slide button to move to Slide 5.

2. Right-click the word *Sirvey* in the title area to display the object menu shown at the top of the next page.

File management

With PowerPoint 97, you can manage your files from within the PowerPoint program. You can delete, rename, or move your files from PowerPoint's Save As or Open dialog box by right-clicking a filename and choosing from several object-menu commands.

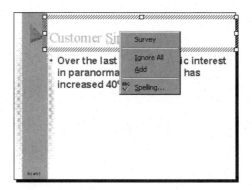

PowerPoint displays at the top of the object menu any words in its dictionary that resemble the misspelled word. You can select one of these words, ignore the misspelling, add the word to PowerPoint's dictionary so that the program will always recognize this word, or move to the Spelling dialog box for more options.

3. Click *Survey* to change the word to its correct spelling.

If we prefer to check the spelling of a presentation all at once, we can use PowerPoint's spell-checking capabilities in another way. Follow these steps:

The Spelling button

1. Move to Slide 1 and click the Spelling button on the Standard toolbar. PowerPoint starts spell-checking the presentation, stops on *Peushin*, and displays this dialog box:

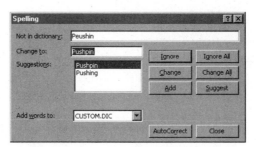

Possible substitutes for *Peushin* appear in the Suggestions list, with the closest match to the unrecognized word displayed in the Change To edit box.

2. This spelling is correct, so click Ignore All to tell PowerPoint that you want to disregard all occurrences of this name.

3. PowerPoint stops on *Gulliver's*, the name of the travel agency. Click Ignore All again.

4. Next PowerPoint stops on *paranormalism*, which is spelled correctly but is not recognized by PowerPoint. Click Add to include *paranormalism* in PowerPoint's dictionary.

5. PowerPoint stops on *dekade*, which is a genuine misspelling. Be sure *decade* appears in the Change To edit box and then click Change.

6. PowerPoint stops on *Toor*, which is also a misspelling. Click *Tour* in the Suggestions list and click Change.

7. When PowerPoint reaches the end of the presentation, it closes the Spelling dialog box and displays a message that the spelling check is complete. Click OK to return to the presentation.

More Editing Techniques

The spell check helped clean up several errors. However, the presentation could still use a little editing. In this section, we'll show you some more ways to make editorial changes to a presentation.

Moving and Copying Text on Slides

Like most other Windows 95 applications, PowerPoint provides two methods for moving text. The first method involves cutting and pasting, which is useful for moving text from one slide to another. The second method involves dragging and dropping, which is useful for moving text on the same slide. Similarly, two methods are provided for copying text.

As a demonstration, let's experiment with the text of Paranormal Tours. Follow these steps:

1. Point to the scroll box in the right scroll bar, hold down the left mouse button, and drag the box to the top of the scroll bar. As you drag, PowerPoint indicates which slide will be displayed if you release the mouse button at that point. Release the mouse button when *Slide: 1 of 8 Paranormal Tours* is displayed.

PowerPoint's dictionaries

PowerPoint checks your spelling by comparing each word in the presentation with those in its built-in dictionary and the CUS-TOM.DIC supplemental dictionary. It flags words that are not in either dictionary with red, wavy underlines. You cannot change the built-in dictionary, but you can add words you use frequently to CUSTOM.DIC, by clicking the Add button in the Spelling dialog box. You can also create special-purpose dictionaries using Notepad, a program that ships with Windows 95. In Notepad, type each word you want to include on a separate line and save the text-only file in the C:\Program Files\Common Files\Microsoft Shared\Proof folder with the extension DIC. To use the special dictionary, select it from the Add Words To list when the Spelling dialog box appears. PowerPoint then checks the words in the presentation against its built-in dictionary and the special-purpose dictionary.

2. Press the PageDown key twice to move to Slide 3, the first slide that needs editing.

The Cut button

3. Select the text of the last bulleted item on the slide. Then click the Cut button on the Standard toolbar, or right-click the selection and choose Cut from the object menu. The text is removed from the slide and stored temporarily on the Windows Clipboard (see the tip below). If you want to copy this text instead of moving it, click the Copy button or choose the Copy command.

The Copy button

4. Move to Slide 2, click an insertion point after the second bulleted item, and press Enter to add a third bullet.

The Paste button

5. Click the Paste button on the Standard toolbar, or right-click the third bullet and then choose the Paste command from the object menu.

6. Edit the text to read *To create tour packages that are flexible*.

Now try dragging and dropping:

Drag-and-drop editing

1. Return to Slide 3, and in the first bulleted item, double-click *insightful* to select it.

2. Point to the selection, hold down the left mouse button, and drag to the end of the first bulleted item, releasing the mouse button when the shadow insertion point is to the right of the last *e* in *enjoyable*. PowerPoint moves the selection to the end of the line, adjusting the spaces appropriately.

3. Next select the word *enjoyable* in the first bulleted item, point to the selection, hold down the left mouse button, and drag

Moving and copying with the keyboard

To use the keyboard to cut text, select the text and press Ctrl+X. Then to paste it, click an insertion point and press Ctrl+V. To copy text instead of moving it, follow the same procedure but use Ctrl+C instead of Ctrl+X.

The Clipboard

The Clipboard temporarily stores cut or copied data from all Windows applications. Because the Clipboard is a temporary storage place, turning off your computer erases any information stored there. You can use the Clipboard to transfer data from one file to another in the same application or from one application to another. Each item you cut or copy overwrites the previous item. To preserve information already on the Clipboard, you can use drag-and-drop editing techniques, which don't use this temporary storage area.

the shadow insertion point to the left of the *b* in *but*. After you release the mouse button, click anywhere to remove the highlight. Here are the results:

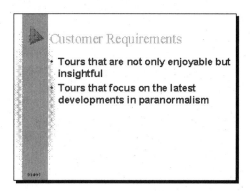

To copy text using drag-and-drop, hold down the Ctrl key while dragging the selection.

Now let's use drag-and-drop with a "twist":

1. Move to Slide 8 and select *worldwide* in the bulleted item.

2. Point to the selection, hold down the right mouse button, and drag to the end of the bulleted item. When you release the mouse button, the object menu shown here appears:

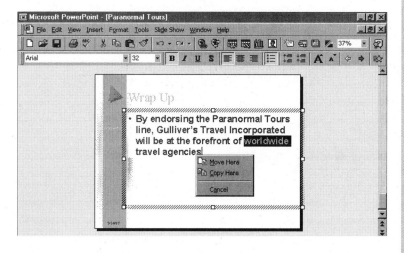

3. Choose Move Here from the menu to relocate the selection.

4. Save the presentation.

AutoCorrect

PowerPoint's AutoCorrect feature corrects simple typos as you enter text on a slide. For example, if you type *teh*, AutoCorrect automatically replaces it with *the*. By default, AutoCorrect also corrects two initial capital letters, such as *TRavel*, and capitalizes the names of days. To include your own commonly misspelled entries in AutoCorrect, choose AutoCorrect from the Tools menu. When the AutoCorrect dialog box appears, type the misspelling in the Replace edit box, type the correct spelling in the With edit box, and click Add. AutoCorrect adds the new entry to its list of common misspellings. (You might want to peruse this list to get a feel for the kinds of words and symbols AutoCorrect fixes by default.) You can delete entries from Auto-Correct's list by selecting the entry and clicking the Delete button. To turn the AutoCorrect feature off, select the Replace Text As You Type option in the Auto-Correct dialog box.

Moving and Copying Text Between Presentations

We've shown you how to move and copy text in the same presentation, and as you'll see if you follow these steps, moving and copying between presentations is equally easy:

1. Display Slide 4 and notice that the Bermuda Triangle Mystery Tour was not included in the bulleted list of sample tours.

2. Choose Sample Tours from the bottom of the Window menu to activate the Sample Tours presentation.

3. Move to Slide 4 and select the slide title, *Bermuda Triangle Mystery Tour*.

4. Click the Copy button on the Formatting toolbar, and then choose Paranormal Tours from the bottom of the Window menu to activate that presentation.

5. With Slide 4 displayed on your screen, click an insertion point after the last bulleted item and press Enter to create a new bulleted item.

6. Without moving the insertion point, click the Paste button on the Standard toolbar to paste the copied text from the Sample Tours presentation. As you can see, the formatting from the slide title has been replaced with the formatting of a bulleted item in this presentation's template.

7. Save Paranormal Tours by clicking the Save button.

To move text between slides in different presentations, simply use the Cut button instead of the Copy button.

Reordering Slide Text in Outline View

We can change the order of bulleted items on a slide by using cut-and-paste techniques in slide view, but reordering items is even simpler in outline view, where we can see all the topics and bulleted lists of the presentation in outline form. We can also edit slide text in outline view, but this view really shines when it's time to organize a presentation. Organizing is often a trial-and-error process. We start by evaluating the major

Repositioning text objects

You can use the mouse to reposition text objects on a slide. For example, if you want to shift the title up a bit, click the title area to select it, point to the frame surrounding the area, hold down the left mouse button, and then drag the frame upward. You can use this same technique to reposition the object area on a slide. In addition, you can resize the objects by dragging the small white squares, called *handles*, that appear when an object is selected.

topics, add and delete a few subtopics, and then move items around and change their levels. This task is easiest to accomplish in outline view because the Outlining toolbar puts the tools needed for organizing a presentation close at hand. Follow these steps:

1. Move to Slide 1 and then click the Outline View button or choose Outline from the View menu.

2. Close the Color slide miniature by clicking its Close button.

3. Scroll the outline until you can see all the bulleted items under the *Some Sample Tours* topic.

4. Click the bullet to the left of *Extraterrestrial Exploration*.

5. Click the Move Up button on the Outlining toolbar until the selected item sits above *Ghostly Bed & Breakfasts*.

The Move Up button

6. Now click the bullet to the left of *Europe* to select the item.

7. Click the Move Down button. *Europe* and *United States* effectively switch places.

The Move Down button

8. Click the bullet to the left of *Ghostly Bed & Breakfasts*. PowerPoint selects not only the text adjacent to the bullet but also its two subordinate items.

9. Click the Move Down button twice. PowerPoint moves the main bullet and its subordinate points to the bottom of the *Some Sample Tours* list, which now looks like this:

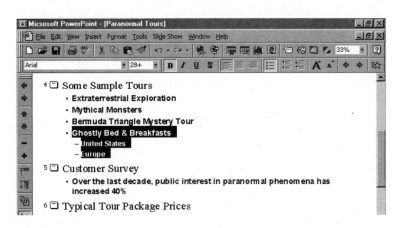

Let's try another method of rearranging bulleted items by following these steps:

1. Scroll the outline until you can see the bulleted items under the *Objectives* topic.

Reordering by dragging

2. Click the bullet to the left of the second bulleted item.

3. Point to the selected text, hold down the left mouse button, drag the shadow insertion point until it sits to the left of the *To* in the first bulleted item, and then release the mouse button. PowerPoint moves the selection to its new location at the top of the bulleted list.

Rearranging a Presentation

When fine-tuning a presentation, we not only need to refine the order of text on each slide but also need to pay attention to the order of the slides themselves. In the following section, we discuss two ways of rearranging the slides of a presentation.

Reordering Slides in Outline View

As you scroll through the presentation's outline, you might notice a slide or two that would work better in a different location. However, if the outline is too long to fit on the screen all at one time, it is sometimes hard to decide on a precise order for the slides. This "can't see the forest for the trees" situation is easily remedied by *collapsing* the outline so that only the main topics are visible. You can then move a topic up or down in the outline to change the order of the presentation's slides. Try this:

The Collapse All button

1. Click the Collapse All button on the Outlining toolbar. Power-Point hides all the bulleted items and puts a gray line under some of the topics to indicate the presence of hidden information, as shown at the top of the facing page.

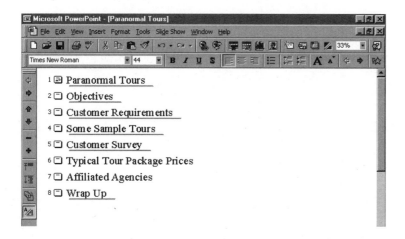

2. Click the slide icon for Slide 5 to select the slide topic and its hidden text, and then click the Move Up button once. *Customer Survey* is now the fourth slide in the outline.

3. Verify that the hidden text moved with the topic by clicking the Expand button on the Outlining toolbar to see this result:

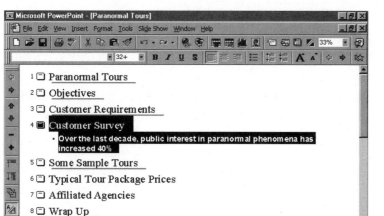

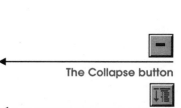

The Expand button

4. Click the Collapse button to once again hide the bulleted item.

The Collapse button

5. To redisplay the entire outline in its new order, click the Expand All button. Then save the presentation.

The Expand All button

Reordering Slides in Slide Sorter View

We've worked on individual slides in slide view and on the presentation outline in outline view. Now let's look at the slides from a different perspective. Slide sorter view gives us a visual overview of the presentation, where we can address issues such as slide sequencing. Here's how to rearrange slides in slide sorter view:

The Slide Sorter View button

1. Press Ctrl+Home to move to the first slide, and then click the Slide Sorter View button in the bottom left corner of the window. When PowerPoint finishes redrawing your screen, it looks like this:

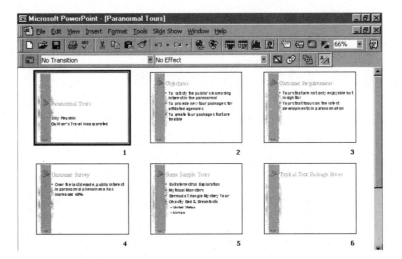

At the top of the screen, PowerPoint has replaced the Formatting toolbar with the Slide Sorter toolbar. (You might want to read the adjacent tip and use ToolTips to familiarize yourself with the buttons on this toolbar.) Thumbnail sketches of the presentation's eight slides are displayed with enough detail to give a good idea of how the slides look. Because you moved to Slide 1 in the outline before clicking the Slide Sorter View button, Slide 1 is selected in slide sorter view, as indicated by the heavy border.

2. Click Slide 4 to select it, point to it, hold down the left mouse button, drag the shadow insertion point (a vertical line) to the left of Slide 3, and then release the mouse button. Slides 3 and 4 switch places.

The Slide Sorter toolbar

You can use the buttons and boxes on the Slide Sorter toolbar to add dynamic effects to an electronic slide show, such as fancy transitions from one slide to the next and slides that "build" themselves one bullet at a time. See Chapter 6 for information about how to add special effects to an electronic slide show.

Changing the Thumbnail Size

Slides 7 and 8 are not visible, making it difficult to work with the entire presentation in this view. Fortunately, we can tell PowerPoint to make the slide thumbnails smaller so that we can see more slides on the screen at the same time. (The smallest size is 20% of full size.) When we work with small thumbnails, it's a good idea to also tell PowerPoint not to bother displaying the slides' formatting. This can be a real time-saver because PowerPoint does not have to "redraw" the slides every time we make a change to the presentation in slide sorter view. Let's experiment:

1. Click the Show Formatting button on the Slide Sorter toolbar to toggle it off. Now the slides display only their titles in black type on a white background.

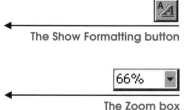

The Show Formatting button

The Zoom box

2. Click the down arrow to the right of the Zoom box on the Standard toolbar, and select 50% from the drop-down list. Your screen now looks like this:

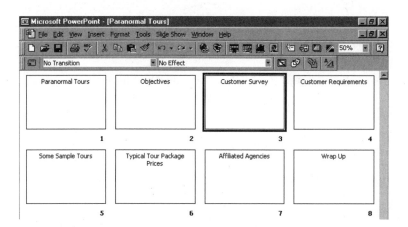

3. Click 50% in the Zoom box to highlight it, type *20*, and press Enter. PowerPoint redraws the thumbnails at 20%.

4. Click the Show Formatting button to redisplay the bulleted items and formatting, and then save and close both presentations.

In Chapter 6, we talk about the other options available on the Slide Sorter toolbar. For now, let's move on to see how to visually display data in a PowerPoint presentation.

3 Presenting Information Visually

In this chapter, we show you how to visually represent data in your presentations. We add and format graphs using Microsoft Graph. Then we create an organization chart using Microsoft Organization Chart. Finally, with the aid of Microsoft Word, we create and edit a table.

We used Microsoft Graph to create and format a graph on Slide 3 of the Paranormal Tours presentation. Then we added an organization chart to Slide 7 using Microsoft Org Chart. Finally, we used Word's table-making capabilities to create and format a table on Slide 6.

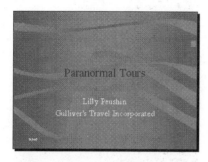

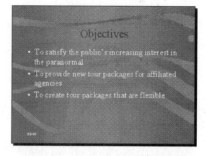

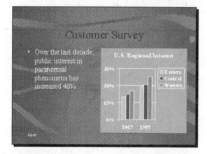

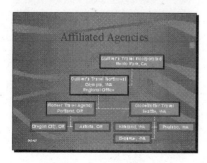

Words are nice, but words alone won't necessarily get our message across. Sometimes we'll need to present facts or figures in a visual format that promotes at-a-glance understanding of trends or relationships. With PowerPoint, we can include a graph to show changes in data over time, add an organization chart to illustrate a company's hierarchy, or create a table to categorize and compare information.

In this chapter, we get down to the real meat and potatoes of presentations by showing you how to add a graph, an organization chart, and a table to the Paranormal Tours presentation.

Adding Graphs

When it comes to presenting numerical data in a clear, concise way, nothing beats a graph. We can use graphs to depict a wide variety of information, from fluctuations in the weather to the value of a stock portfolio. In this section, we show you the ins and outs of using PowerPoint's built-in graphing program, Microsoft Graph, so that you can take full advantage of it for your own presentations. We start by adding a column graph to a slide, and then we show you how to format and manipulate the graph in various ways.

Microsoft Graph

Using a Graph AutoLayout

With PowerPoint, we can add graphs to slides using three methods: we can use a graph autolayout, we can click the Insert Chart button on the Standard toolbar, or we can choose Microsoft Graph from the Insert menu. For this example, we'll change the autolayout of an existing slide of the Paranormal Tours presentation so that it will accommodate both its current text and a graph. Follow these steps:

Bypassing the graph autolayouts

You don't have to change a slide's autolayout in order to add a graph to the slide. Instead, you can use the Insert Chart button on Power-Point's Standard toolbar or the Microsoft Graph command on the Insert menu to add a graph to any slide. First move to the slide in slide view, and click the Insert Chart button or choose Microsoft Graph from the Insert menu. When Microsoft Graph opens, create the graph as described in this chapter.

1. Open Paranormal Tours, click the Apply Design button, and double-click Ribbons to switch to that template.

2. If necessary, click the Slide View button to switch to slide view, and move to Slide 3.

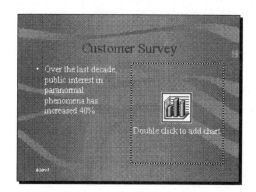

The Slide Layout button

3. Click the Slide Layout button on the Standard toolbar. When the Slide Layout dialog box appears, select the Text & Chart Autolayout (the first autolayout in the second row) and click Apply. Slide 3 now looks like this:

4. Double-click the graph placeholder to start Microsoft Graph. Your screen looks something like this:

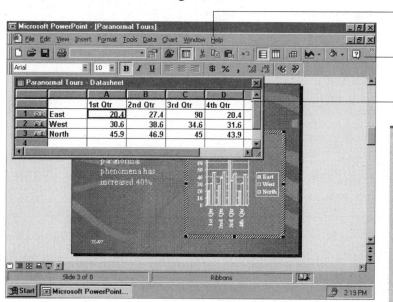

Graph's menu bar

Graph's Standard toolbar

Datasheet with default data

Graph first presents you with its default *datasheet*, which resembles a worksheet in a spreadsheet program. In the leftmost column and topmost row of the datasheet are gray headers that identify the columns by letter and the rows by number. Depending on whether our data is organized by column or by row (see the adjacent tip), one set of headers

By row or by column

You can arrange the data series in a datasheet by row or by column. By default, Graph arranges the series by row; but if you have arranged the series by column, you can ensure that Graph will plot your data correctly by clicking the By Column button on Graph's Standard toolbar. If you want to return to the by-row arrangement, click the By Row button. Graph places miniature markers on the row number buttons of the datasheet if the data series are arranged by row and on the column letter buttons if the data series are arranged by column.

also displays icons that indicate the current graph type (the default is a three-dimensional column graph).

On the white part of the datasheet, we enter the data we want to plot as a graph. Gridlines divide the datasheet into units called *cells*. The first column and first row are reserved for headings called *labels*, which are used to identify information on the graph. We enter data by first clicking a cell to select it and then typing the information. To move to another cell, we can click it with the mouse; use the Arrow keys; or press Enter (to move to the cell below), Shift+Enter (to move to the cell above), Tab (to move to the next cell), or Shift+Tab (to move to the previous cell). We can press Home or End to move to the beginning or end of the current row, or Ctrl+Home or Ctrl+End to move to the beginning or end of the datasheet.

Now that we're acquainted with Graph's datasheet, let's replace its "dummy" data with our own information, starting with the labels:

1. Click the 1st Qtr label in column A. (If you click outside the datasheet or graph, you will return to PowerPoint. Double-click the graph on the current slide to start Graph again.)

2. Type *1987*, press Tab to move to column B, and type *1997*.

3. Click the East label in row 1.

4. Type *Eastern*, press Enter to move to row 2, and type *Central*.

5. Press Enter one more time and type *Western*.

To speed up the entry of the remaining data in the datasheet, try this technique:

1. Point to the second cell in column A, hold down the left mouse button, drag to the fourth cell in column B, and then release the mouse button. The datasheet should look like this:

Adjusting column width

To increase or decrease the width of a column in a datasheet, first select the column. (To select an entire column or row, simply click the corresponding header button. To select the entire datasheet, click the "blank" button located at the intersection of the column letter and row number buttons.) Choose Column Width from Graph's Format menu, and enter a number in the Column Width dialog box. Click the Best Fit button in the Column Width dialog box to automatically adjust the column width to fit the longest entry in the column. You can also use the mouse to change the column width. Simply point to the border that separates adjacent column letter buttons, and when the pointer changes to a vertical bar with two arrows, hold down the left mouse button and drag to the right or left. If you double-click the border between two column letter buttons, the width of the column on the left is automatically adjusted to fit the longest entry. You can select multiple columns, and use any of the methods described above to change the width of all the selected columns simultaneously.

Paranormal Tours - Datasheet		A	B	C	D	
		1987	1997	3rd Qtr	4th Qtr	
1	Eastern	20.4	27.4	90	20.4	
2	Central	30.6	38.6	34.6	31.6	
3	Western	45.9	46.9	45	43.9	
4						

2. Now type *20%*, press Enter, type *22%*, press Enter, type *25%*, and press Enter. In the next column, type *29%*, *31%*, and *38%*, pressing Enter after each number. (By the way, this data is fictitious and is used for demonstration purposes only.)

3. Click the Save button on Graph's Standard toolbar to save your work.

Before we can plot the graph, we must exclude the "dummy" data in columns C and D by following these steps:

1. Click column C's header, hold down the Shift key, click column D's header, and release the Shift key. ◄──────

Excluding data

2. With both columns selected, choose Exclude Row/Col from Graph's Data menu.

3. Click the View Datasheet button on Graph's Standard toolbar ◄────── or choose Datasheet from Graph's View menu to remove the datasheet. The new graph looks like this:

The View Datasheet button

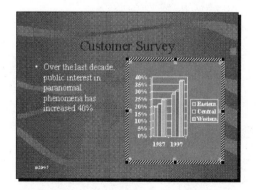

Obviously, we'll have to make some adjustments, such as enlarging and repositioning the graph on the slide.

The Chart Type button

Changing the Graph Type

With Graph, we can easily switch to a different graph type if we don't like the way our data is displayed. For clarity, change the graph type on Slide 3 by following these steps:

1. Click the arrow to the right of the Chart Type button on Graph's Standard toolbar to display this palette of options:

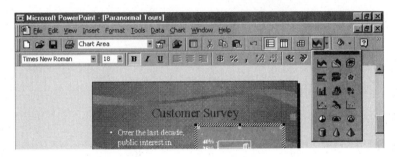

2. Click one of the palette's options and notice the effect on your graph. Try other graph types to get a feel for what's available.

3. When you're ready, click the Line Chart option (the fourth option in the left column) to switch to a line graph. The results are shown here:

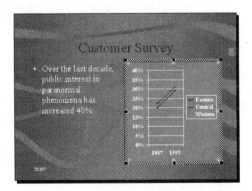

The default graph format

Initially, Graph creates a graph in its default format—a three-dimensional column graph. To change the default format, choose Chart Type from Graph's Chart menu and select a different type on the Standard Types or Custom Types tab of the Chart Type dialog box. Then click the Set As Default Chart button at the bottom of the dialog box, and when PowerPoint displays a message box to confirm your default graph selection, click Yes. After you click OK in the Chart Type dialog box, the new default graph type takes effect immediately and remains in effect until you change it.

Here's a more flexible way of switching graph types:

1. Choose Chart Type from Graph's Chart menu to display the Chart Type dialog box shown on the facing page, where the current type is highlighted.

On the Standard Types tab, the box on the left lists all the available graph types, and the sub-types for the selected graph type are displayed on the right. Clicking a sub-type displays its description in the box below.

2. Click the Custom Types tab to display these options:

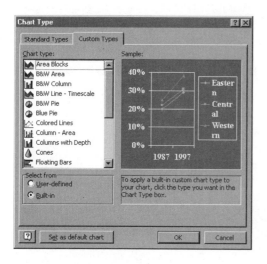

If none of the standard graph types fits the bill, PowerPoint provides 20 custom graph types, including combination graphs (see the adjacent tip).

3. Explore the graph types available on both the Custom Types and Standard Types tabs.

Combination graphs

To create a combination graph, select one of the combination graph types on the Custom Types tab of the Chart Type dialog box. You can plot your data as one graph type overlaid by another graph type—for example, a column graph overlaid by a line graph. Or if your data includes series that span widely divergent ranges of values, you can plot one data series against a y-axis scale on the left side of the graph and another data series against a y-axis scale on the right side of the graph.

4. When you finish exploring, select Column on the Standard
Types tab, select the two-dimensional clustered column sub-
type, and click OK to close the Chart Type dialog box and
return to Slide 3 with the chart redrawn according to your
instructions.

Working with Graph Objects

Before we can make any adjustments to a graph, we must
select the graph object we want to change. If Graph is still
open, we can select a graph object by simply clicking it with
the mouse. Colored squares, called *handles*, surround the
object to indicate that it is selected. If we are working in
PowerPoint, we can quickly start Graph by double-clicking
the current graph or by clicking the graph once and pressing
Enter. We can then click the graph object we want to modify.

The Format button

After we select a graph object, we can choose the Selected
Object command from Graph's Format menu to open a dialog
box with options related to the selected object. We can also
open the Format dialog box by clicking the Format button on
Graph's Standard toolbar; by right-clicking a graph object
and choosing the Format *Object* command from the object
menu; or by double-clicking the graph object.

If you're a little baffled by all this, don't worry: we'll walk
you through the entire process in a moment. Before we do,
however, take a minute or two to study the following figure,
which depicts the graph objects on a typical graph:

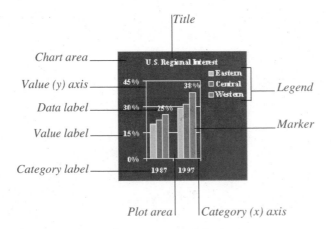

Adding and Formatting a Title

We can add a title to the graph, the category (x) axis, the value (y) axis, or all three. We can then format the title or titles using the Format dialog box. Try this:

1. With Graph open (if it isn't, double-click the column graph on Slide 3 to start the program), choose Chart Options from Graph's Chart menu, and if necessary, click the Titles tab to display these options:

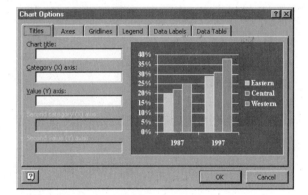

2. In the Chart Title edit box, type *U.S. Regional Interest* and check the new title in the preview box. Then click OK.

3. With the title selected (surrounded by handles), choose Selected Chart Title from Graph's Format menu to display this dialog box:

Formatting a graph title

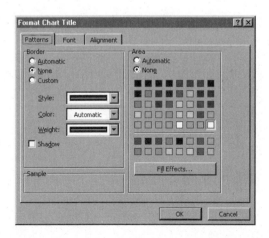

Adding an axis title

To add a title to a graph's axis, choose the Chart Options command from Graph's Chart menu, enter a title in the appropriate edit box on the Titles tab of the Chart Options dialog box, and click OK. You can then rotate the selected title by choosing Selected Axis Title from Graph's Format menu, clicking the Alignment tab of the Format Axis Title dialog box, and changing the Degrees setting in the Orientation section.

4. Click the Alignment tab, select Top from the Vertical drop-down list, and click OK. The title shifts upward in its box.

Adding and Formatting Legends

By default, Graph added a legend to the column graph in Paranormal Tours. If a graph does not have a legend, we can add one on the Legend tab of the Chart Options dialog box. To remove a legend, simply select it and press the Delete key.

Because a legend is a graph object, we can format it using the same techniques described for other graph objects. We can: select the legend and then choose Selected Legend from Graph's Format menu; right-click the legend and choose Format Legend from the object menu; or double-click the legend. When the Format Legend dialog box appears, use the options on the Patterns, Font, and Placement tabs to change the border, background, font, location, and size of the legend.

As well as using the Placement tab to reposition and resize the legend, we can use the mouse. Follow these steps:

1. Click the legend once to select it. (Be sure the entire legend is selected, not one of the legend entries or keys.)

Repositioning a legend →

2. Point to the border surrounding the legend (not a handle), hold down the left mouse button, drag upward until the legend is aligned with the graph's top gridline, and then release the mouse button.

3. Click anywhere in the chart area to deselect the legend. (Be careful not to click *outside* the chart area, or you'll wind up back in PowerPoint.) The graph now looks like this:

Formatting parts of a legend

You can select an entry in a legend (such as *Eastern* in the sample column graph's legend) and change its font, font style, size, and so on using the Format Legend dialog box. And if that's not enough, you can even select a legend key (the small color box next to each legend entry) and change its border, color, and background using the Format Legend Key dialog box.

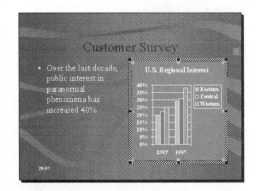

Adding and Formatting Axes, Tick Marks, Gridlines, and Labels

The two-dimensional column graph in Paranormal Tours has two axes: the *value* or vertical y axis and the *category* or horizontal x axis. Logically, values are plotted along the value axis, and categories are plotted along the category axis. You'll find axes in all the graph types except pie and doughnut graphs. Some three-dimensional graph types, such as three-dimensional area, three-dimensional column, three-dimensional line, and three-dimensional surface graphs, have a third axis, called the *series* axis. In these graphs, the x axis remains the category axis, the y axis becomes the series axis, and the z axis becomes the value axis.

This may all sound a bit confusing, but the figures shown below should help clarify matters. The figure on the left is a two-dimensional column graph with category (x) and value (y) axes. The figure on the right is a three-dimensional column graph with category (x), series (y), and value (z) axes. Note that the three-dimensional column graph has additional graph objects called the *walls* and the *floor* and that the value axis rises up from the floor while the category and series axes are plotted along the floor.

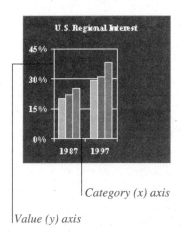

Category (x) axis

Value (y) axis

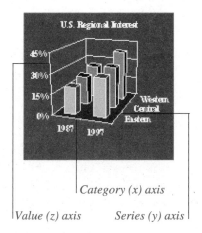

Category (x) axis

Value (z) axis   *Series (y) axis*

The small marks used to group values or categories along the axes are called *tick marks*. A graph can have major tick marks and minor tick marks, but only major tick marks appear by default. To add minor tick marks, select the axis, choose

Selected Axis from Graph's Format menu, and then select one of the Minor Tick Mark Type options on the Patterns tab of the Format Axis dialog box. We can also use options on the Patterns tab to remove or reposition the major tick marks along the selected axis.

In some cases, gridlines can help make a graph more readable. The current graph has gridlines emanating from the major tick marks along the value axis, allowing us to more easily assess the values of the data markers. We can add gridlines to both major and minor tick marks by selecting from the options on the Gridlines tab of the Chart Options dialog box. After we've added gridlines, we can format them by selecting a gridline along one axis, choosing Selected Gridlines from Graph's Format menu, and then using the Patterns tab of the Format Gridlines dialog box to change the style, color, and weight of all the gridlines or the Scale tab to change the scale. (We'll change the scale in a moment.) We can remove gridlines from a graph by deselecting the appropriate options on the Gridlines tab of the Chart Options dialog box.

The column graph in Paranormal Tours sports labels along both axes. We can change the position (see the adjacent tip), font, number format (see the tip on page 68), and alignment of the labels by selecting their corresponding axis, choosing Selected Axis from Graph's Format menu, and then selecting options in the Format Axis dialog box.

For example, the value axis labels are a bit crowded. To reduce the crowding, we can change the scale of the axis, like this:

1. Click the arrow to the right of the Chart Objects box on Graph's Standard toolbar and select Value Axis from the drop-down list. (This method of selecting a graph object is particularly helpful for graph objects that are difficult to select with the mouse.)

2. Choose Selected Axis from the Format menu and click the Scale tab of the Format Axis dialog box to display the options shown on the facing page.

Changing label position

By default, Graph places tick-mark labels next to their respective axes. You can change the position of the labels by selecting one of the Tick-Mark Labels options on the Patterns tab of the Format Axis dialog box. (To open this dialog box, select an axis and then choose Selected Axis from Graph's Format menu.) Selecting the Low or High option places labels next to the minimum or maximum values. Selecting the None option removes the labels altogether.

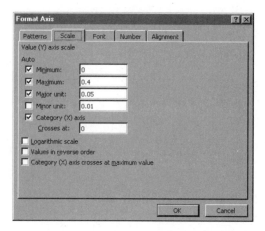

3. Under Auto, you can see that the value axis is scaled from 0 to 0.4, with a label at major-unit intervals of 0.05. Double-click the Major Unit edit box, type *0.15* to display four labels along the value axis instead of nine, and click OK.

4. Click outside the graph to see these results in PowerPoint:

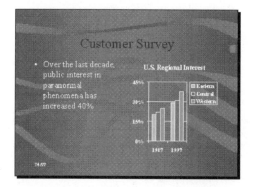

Formatting the Chart and Plot Areas

To give the chart area a little more distinction, we can add a border to it and change its background color. (We can use the same techniques to format the plot area.) And, rather than change the formatting of individual text elements on the graph, such as the title and tick-mark labels, we can save some time by changing the formatting of all the text at once in the Format Chart Area dialog box. Follow the steps on the next page to add a border, change the background color, and format the text of the column graph in Paranormal Tours.

Adding data labels

You can add labels to data series markers to show the value or percent of each marker. Double-click one of the data markers to display the Format Data Series dialog box, click the Data Labels tab, select the Show Value or Show Percent option, and then click OK. You can then format the data labels by selecting a label or labels, choosing Selected Data Labels from Graph's Format menu, and then selecting options in the Format Data Labels dialog box.

Adding a border ──────────▶ 1. Start Graph and double-click the chart area (the blank area below the legend is a good spot). Graph displays the Format Chart Area dialog box.

2. On the Patterns tab, click the arrow to the right of the Color box in the Border section to display a color palette, and then select the Yellow box in the fourth row of the palette.

3. Next, click the arrow to the right of the Weight box and select the last option (heavy).

4. Click the Shadow check box to give the border a shadow.

Changing the background ──────▶
color
5. To change the color of the chart area's background, move to the Area section of the Patterns tab and select the fifth (green) box from the left in the second row of the color palette.

Changing the font and ──────▶
font style
6. If we wanted to change the font and font style of all the text on the graph, we could click the Font tab and make our selections. But the font settings are fine as they are, so click OK to close the dialog box.

7. Click anywhere outside the graph to return to PowerPoint, and then click anywhere outside Slide 3 to deselect the graph. Here are the results:

Formatting numbers

To change the formatting of numeric tick-mark labels, you can use the options on the Number tab of the Format Axis dialog box. If the Linked To Source option is selected, the numbers have the same formatting as the numbers in the datasheet. To apply a different format, select an option from the Category list, and then select the format you want from the list on the right. A sample of your selection appears at the top of the Number tab. You can create a custom format by selecting the Custom option in the Category list and entering the appropriate codes in the Type edit box.

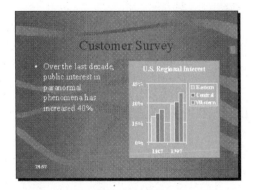

Moving and Sizing Graphs in PowerPoint

We don't have to open Microsoft Graph in order to move and resize the chart area of a graph. We can accomplish these tasks in PowerPoint, like this:

1. Choose Ruler from the View menu to turn on PowerPoint's rulers. (The rulers will serve as guides when you move and resize the graph.)

Displaying the rulers

2. Click the column graph in Paranormal Tours once to select it.

3. Point inside the graph's border, hold down the left mouse button, and when the dashed positioning box appears, drag to the left about ¼ inch, using the horizontal ruler as a guide, and release the mouse button.

4. To increase the width of the graph, point to the right center handle, and when the pointer changes to a double-headed arrow, hold down the left mouse button, and drag to the right about ½ inch.

5. If necessary, drag the bottom border of the graph down a bit to give the category axis labels some breathing room.

6. Choose Ruler from the View menu to turn off the rulers and then deselect the graph to see these results:

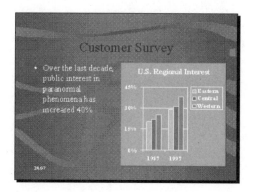

Adding Organization Charts

Adding graphs to our slides isn't the only way to include visual information in our presentations. If you flip back to page 55, you'll see an organization chart, henceforth known as *org charts*, on Slide 7 of the Paranormal Tours presentation. Org charts are useful for showing hierarchies, such as the executive branch of a corporation where the CEO occupies the top position and a president, vice presidents, and so

Adding text boxes and arrows

To embellish your graph with text, display the Drawing toolbar, and click the Text Box button on the Drawing toolbar. Then position the cross-hair pointer where you want the text box to appear, hold down the left mouse button, and drag to create the box. A flashing insertion point appears inside the text box so that you can enter text, and as you type, the text automatically wraps within the invisible boundaries of the box. To reposition a text box, place the mouse pointer on the box's border, hold down the left mouse button, and drag to a new location. To resize a text box, drag one of its handles. To delete a text box, select it and press Delete. You can also connect a text box to an item in your graph by drawing an arrow. Click the Arrow button on the Drawing toolbar, position the mouse pointer at the starting point for the arrow, hold down the left mouse button, and drag to the ending point for the arrow. Like other graph objects, you can format text boxes and arrows by using the options in the Format *Object* dialog box.

on, occupy subordinate positions. However, the basic organization chart elements can also be used to develop flow charts that illustrate processes.

Here's how to create Slide 7's org chart:

1. With Paranormal Tours open, move to Slide 7.

2. Click the Slide Layout button on the Standard toolbar, and then double-click the Organization Chart autolayout (the third autolayout in the second row) in the Slide Layout dialog box. PowerPoint adds an org chart placeholder to the object area.

3. Double-click the placeholder to open the Microsoft Organization Chart program. Your screen should now look like this:

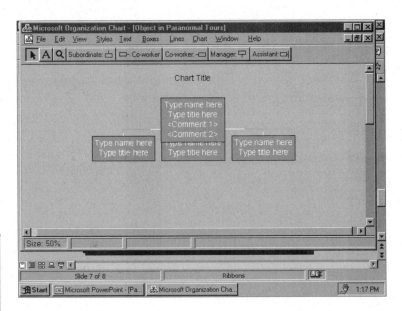

Another way to add an org chart

You don't have to change a slide's layout in order to add an org chart to the slide. Display the slide in slide view and choose Object from the Insert menu. When the Insert Object dialog box appears, be sure the Create New option is selected, and then double-click the MS Organization Chart 2.0 option in the Object Type list. When the Org Chart program opens, complete the org chart as described in this chapter.

As you can see, the Org Chart window has its own menu bar, toolbar, and status bar. You use commands and buttons to create an org chart and then add it to a PowerPoint slide.

4. Click the Maximize button at the right end of the Org Chart window's title bar to maximize the window.

5. Because the slide already has a title, select the text of the chart title placeholder with the mouse and press Delete.

Now we're ready to fill in the org chart's boxes:

1. Click the topmost box to select it, type *Gulliver's Travel Northwest* as the name, and press Enter.

Filling in the boxes

2. Type *Olympia, WA* as the title, and press Enter.

3. For the first comment, type *Regional Office*, and then click the leftmost subordinate box to select it.

4. Type *Globetrotter Travel*, press Enter, and type *Seattle, WA*.

5. Click the second subordinate box, type *Pioneer Travel Agency*, press Enter, type *Portland, OR*, and click outside the box. Here are the results:

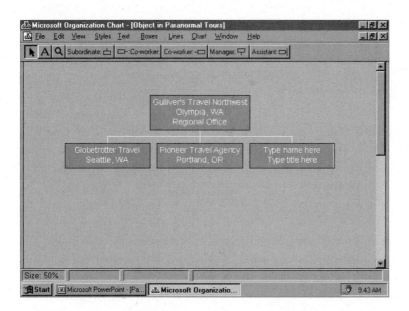

6. Choose the Update Paranormal Tours command from Org Chart's File menu to update the underlying slide.

Updating a presentation

To actually save the org chart as part of the presentation, we must return to PowerPoint and choose Save from Power-Point's File menu. To reopen the Org Chart window, we can simply double-click the org chart in PowerPoint. (To save the org chart as a separate file, we can use the Save Copy As command on Org Chart's File menu.)

Saving an org chart

Adding and Removing Boxes

We aren't limited to the four boxes the Org Chart program has provided. We can add and remove boxes with just a few mouse clicks. Follow these steps:

Manager: ⊡

The Manager button

1. To add a box to the top of the org chart, click the Manager button on the Org Chart toolbar, move the mouse pointer (which is now shaped like a manager box) to the topmost box, and click once.

2. Click the new box, type *Gulliver's Travel Incorporated*, press Enter, and type *Menlo Park, CA*.

Assistant: ⊏⊐

The Assistant button

3. Next, click the Assistant button on the Org Chart toolbar, and click the Gulliver's Travel Northwest box to add an assistant box to the org chart.

4. Click the new box and type *Kirkland, WA*.

Subordinate: ⊏⊐

The Subordinate button

5. Add two subordinate boxes to Globetrotter Travel by clicking the Subordinate button on the Org Chart toolbar twice (the status bar displays *Create: 2*), moving the mouse pointer to the Globetrotter Travel box, and clicking once. Org Chart draws the two boxes below the Globetrotter Travel box.

Changing org chart defaults

Use the Options command on Org Chart's Edit menu to change the default settings for org charts. The 4-Box Template option (the default setting) displays the org chart template with four boxes every time you open a new org chart. The 1-Box Template option displays the org chart template with one box, and the Topmost Box option displays the org chart template with one box and the formatting of the org chart that was active when you selected the option. If you want Org Chart to use the same magnification every time you open a new org chart, select the Current Magnification option (see page 75 for more information about magnification).

6. In the new subordinate boxes, type *Poulsbo, WA* and then *Bellevue, WA*.

7. Repeat steps 5 and 6 to add two subordinate boxes to Pioneer Travel Agency, and then type *Oregon City, OR* and *Astoria, OR* in the boxes. (Use the scroll bars to scroll the boxes into view, if necessary.)

8. Remove the extraneous box to the right of the Pioneer Travel Agency box by selecting it and then pressing the Delete key. Your org chart now looks like the one shown at the top of the facing page.

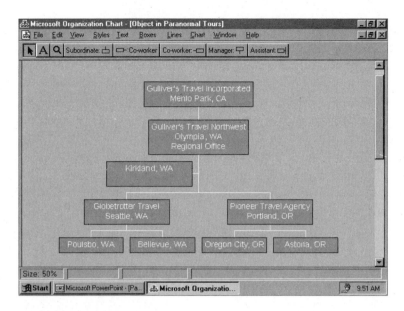

Rearranging Boxes

If we're not happy with the present arrangement of boxes in an org chart, we can use the mouse to rearrange them in a variety of ways. Let's rearrange some of our boxes now:

1. Point to the Pioneer Travel Agency box, hold down the left mouse button, and then drag the box's frame over the Globetrotter Travel box.

2. When the pointer changes to a left-pointing arrow, release the mouse button. The Globetrotter Travel and Pioneer Travel Agency boxes switch places. (Notice that the subordinate boxes below Pioneer Travel Agency have moved as well.)

As you've seen, the shape of the mouse pointer indicates the new position. A left-pointing arrow indicates that the box will appear to the left of the existing box; a right-pointing arrow indicates that the box will appear to the right; and a subordinate box indicates that the box will appear below the existing one. Try the following:

1. Drag the Kirkland, WA box's frame over the Globetrotter Travel box, move slowly downward until the pointer changes to a subordinate box, and release the mouse button.

Org chart size

Bear in mind the size of your slide when you create an org chart. If the org chart is too small, viewers may not be able to read the contents of the boxes. If the org chart consists of many boxes, consider breaking it into logical sections and placing them on separate slides so that viewers aren't overwhelmed with information.

2. Click outside the Kirkland, WA box to deselect it. Then drag the box to the left of the Poulsbo, WA box. Here are the results:

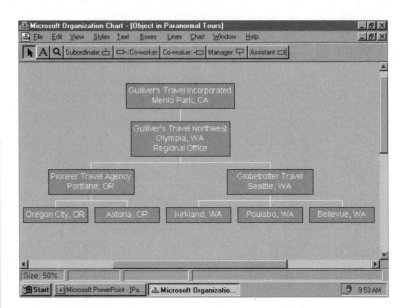

Selecting in org charts

To change the style of a group or branch, you must first select it. To select a group, you can select one member of the group and then press Ctrl+G; you can choose Select and then Group from Org Chart's Edit menu; or you can use the selection tool on the Org Chart toolbar to draw a selection box around the group. Similarly, to select a branch, you can select one member of the branch and then press Ctrl+B; you can choose Select and then Branch from Org Chart's Edit menu; or you can use the selection tool to draw a selection box around it. In addition to the Select commands on Org Chart's Edit menu, you can use the Select Levels command to select all the boxes at a specified level in your org chart. When you choose this command from the Edit menu, Org Chart displays the Select Levels dialog box, in which you enter the relevant org chart levels. For example, if your org chart has four levels and you want to select the first three, type *1* in the first edit box, then type *3* in the second edit box, and click OK.

Switching Styles

Before we get into a discussion about styles, you need to become familiar with some terminology. In Org Chart jargon, a *group* refers to the subordinates under a manager, and a *branch* refers to a manager plus all subordinates. By default, groups are placed side by side in boxes, as in the sample org chart; however, the Org Chart program offers several style alternatives for both groups and branches.

Experiment with some of the other org chart styles by following these steps:

1. Select the Kirkland, WA box and press Ctrl+G. All three Globetrotter Travel subordinate boxes are now selected.

2. From Org Chart's Styles menu, choose the second style in the first row. The org chart looks like the one shown at the top of the facing page.

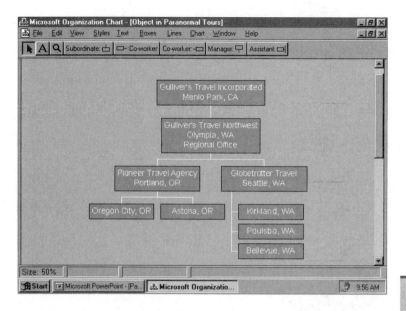

3. The pointer can be used as a *selection tool* to choose more than one box. To see how, point above and to the left of the Oregon City, OR box, hold down the left mouse button, and drag a selection box around the two subordinates of Pioneer Travel Agency. (To select boxes using this method, the selection box must completely enclose them.)

4. If two or more members of an organization share the same manager as well as the same responsibilities, those members can be designated as co-managers. To designate the selected boxes as co-managers, choose the Co-Manager style from Org Chart's Styles menu by clicking its icon.

Now let's condense the org chart by changing the style of its main branch:

1. With any box selected, choose Select and then All from Org Chart's Edit menu.

2. From Org Chart's Styles menu, choose the third style in the first row. The results are shown on the next page.

Magnifying an org chart

You can use the commands on Org Chart's View menu to adjust the magnification of an org chart: The following are the available commands:

- Size To Window displays the entire org chart, fitted to fill the Org Chart window.

- 50% Of Actual, or half the size of a slide, offers a balance of overview and text legibility.

- Actual Size displays the org chart at 50% larger than its printed size, giving the visual effect of a live slide show.

- 200% Of Actual, or double the size of a slide, is useful for examining your work at the greatest level of detail.

You can also use the Zoom button on the Org Chart toolbar (the button with the magnifier icon) to enlarge areas of the org chart. To return to the previous magnification, click the Zoom button again to toggle it off (it now displays an org chart icon) and then click anywhere in the org chart.

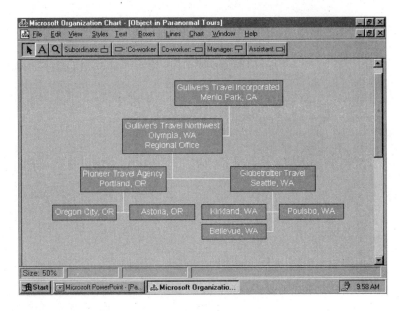

Formatting an Org Chart

We can format the text, boxes, and lines in an org chart by using the commands on Org Chart's Text and Boxes menus. In the following sections, we spruce up each of these components with a bit of formatting.

Formatting Org Chart Text

Org Chart's Text menu provides commands for changing the font, color, and alignment of an org chart's text. The alignment commands—Left, Right, and Center (the default)—are self-explanatory; but let's see how to change the font style and size of the text in the org chart so that it really stands out:

Changing the font

1. Be sure the entire org chart is selected. If it isn't, press Ctrl+A.

2. Choose Font from Org Chart's Text menu, and when the Font dialog box appears, select Bold in the Font Style list, select 18 in the Size list, and click OK.

Formatting Org Chart Boxes

We can use the commands on the Boxes menu to format the org chart boxes in a variety of ways. Follow the steps on the facing page.

1. If necessary, press Ctrl+A to select all the boxes in the org chart, and choose Border Style from Org Chart's Boxes menu to display this list of border options:

Changing the border style

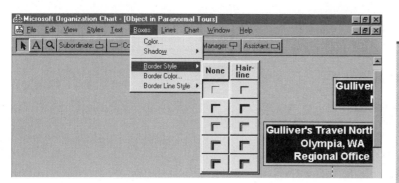

2. Select the fourth border option in the second column.

3. Next, choose Shadow from Org Chart's Boxes menu to display this list of shadow options:

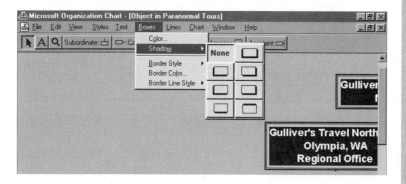

4. Select the second shadow option in the second column.

Formatting Org Chart Lines

Three commands on Org Chart's Lines menu change the thickness, style, and color of the connecting lines in an org chart. Try this:

1. Choose Select and then Connecting Lines from Org Chart's Edit menu.

2. Choose Thickness from Org Chart's Lines menu and select the third line option to increase the thickness of the lines.

Drawing lines and boxes

You'll find four drawing tools at the right end of the Org Chart toolbar. (If you don't see the tools, choose the Show Draw Tools command from Org Chart's View menu.) If Org Chart's built-in box arrangements don't quite satisfy your requirements, you can use these tools to draw lines and boxes exactly where they're needed. For example, you use the first two tools to draw perpendicular and diagonal lines. The third tool draws connecting lines, and the fourth tool draws boxes. To use a drawing tool, click it, position the mouse pointer at the starting point for the line or box, hold down the left mouse button, and drag to the ending point for the line or box. (When you use the Auxiliary Line tool, you must drag from the edge of one existing box to the edge of another existing box.) You can resize a line or box by selecting it and dragging its handles, and you can reposition a line or box by placing the mouse pointer on the line or box border, holding down the left mouse button, and dragging to a new location on the org chart. Lines and boxes created with the drawing tools are actually part of the org chart's background, and they remain stationary when you move or resize the org chart itself. So you should finalize the org chart before you draw lines or boxes.

3. With all the lines still selected, choose Style from Org Chart's Lines menu and select the last (dashed) line option.

4. Click anywhere outside the Org Chart to deselect the connecting lines, and scroll the window to see these results:

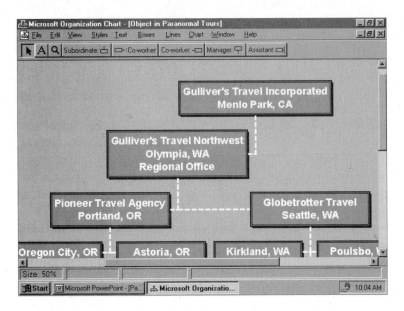

Returning to PowerPoint

After an org chart is complete, quitting Org Chart and returning to PowerPoint automatically adds the org chart to the current slide. Once the org chart is in place, we can use the mouse to reposition or resize it. (We can return to the Org Chart program at any time by double-clicking the org chart on the slide.) Follow these steps to return to PowerPoint:

1. Choose Update Paranormal Tours from Org Chart's File menu. (If you don't choose this command first, you will be prompted to update the org chart before proceeding.)

2. Choose the Exit And Return To Paranormal Tours command from Org Chart's File menu.

Back in PowerPoint, you can see that the org chart definitely needs to be enlarged. Follow these steps:

1. Be sure the org chart is selected (surrounded by handles). If it isn't, click the object area once to select the org chart.

Selecting lines

Before you can change lines in an org chart, you must select them. To select a single connecting line, simply click it with the mouse. To select multiple lines, hold down the Shift key as you click each line, or choose Select and then Connecting Lines from Org Chart's Edit menu. You know a line is selected when it is dotted. (If you happen to select org chart boxes as well as lines when using the first method, any changes you make using the commands on the Line menu also affect the borders of the boxes.)

2. Drag the corner handles to enlarge the height and width proportionally until the org chart fills the slide, like this:

Sizing an org chart

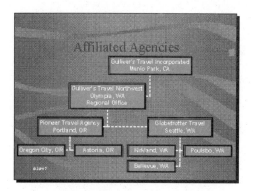

Adding Tables

Adding tables to PowerPoint slides is a snap as long as you also have Microsoft Word 97. Unlike graphs and org charts, whose source programs are included with PowerPoint, tables can be created only by borrowing Word's table-making capabilities (or by importing tables from another application, which is a topic beyond the scope of this book).

In the following sections, we'll show you how to add a table to a slide, enter data, modify the table's structure, and format the table. We've got a lot to do, so let's get started:

1. With the Paranormal Tours presentation open in slide view, move to Slide 6.

2. Click the Slide Layout button on the Standard toolbar and double-click the Table autolayout (the fourth autolayout in the first row).

Creating a table slide

3. Double-click the table placeholder in the object area of the slide to display this dialog box:

Specifying the number of
columns and rows

4. Type *4* in the Number Of Columns edit box, double-click the Number Of Rows edit box, type *5*, and click OK. Word's menu bar and toolbars replace PowerPoint's, and an empty table with the number of columns and rows you specified appears, like this:

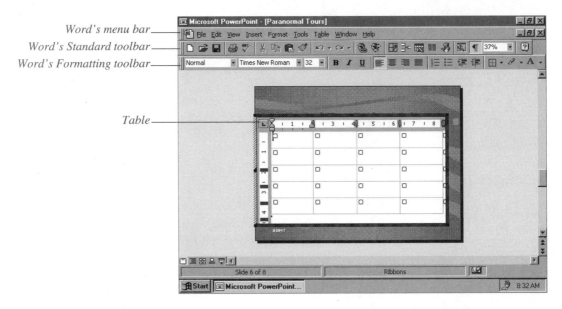

Word's menu bar
Word's Standard toolbar
Word's Formatting toolbar
Table

Like the datasheet in Graph (see page 57), the table is divided into units called *cells*. The gridlines that demarcate the cells can be turned on and off by choosing Hide/Show Gridlines from Word's Table menu. (These gridlines do not appear on the actual slide.) An insertion point rests in the first cell of the table, just to the left of a circular end-of-cell marker. Similar end-of-row markers designate the end of each row in the table. (If you don't see these markers, click the Show/Hide ¶ button on the Standard toolbar.)

Another way to add a table

You don't have to change a slide's autolayout in order to add a table to a slide. Instead, you can use the Insert Microsoft Word Table button on PowerPoint's Standard toolbar to add a table to any slide. First display the slide in slide view and click the Insert Microsoft Word Table button to drop down a table grid. Drag across the number of columns and down the number of rows you want. When you release the mouse button, the specified table opens in Word. You can then complete the table as described in this chapter.

5. If rulers appear across the top and down the left side of the table, choose Ruler from the View menu to turn them off. (You don't need the rulers right now.)

Entering Data

We enter data in a table the same way we enter data elsewhere in PowerPoint: by typing it. We can move the insertion point to a cell by clicking the cell with the mouse or by using the keys and key combinations listed in the table at the top of the facing page.

Key(s)	Moves insertion point
Up or Down Arrow	Up or down one line or cell
Left or Right Arrow	Left or right one character or cell
Tab or Shift+Tab	To next or previous cell
Alt+Home or Alt+End	To first or last cell in current row
Alt+PageUp or Alt+PageDown	To first or last cell in current column

If you make a mistake, use the Backspace or Delete key; and if you want to start a new paragraph within a cell, use the Enter key. Try the following:

1. With the insertion point located in the first cell of the table, type *Tour*, and press Tab. Type *Airfare*, press Tab, and type *Transport*.

2. In the second cell of the first column, type *ET Exploration*, press Tab, type *$200*, press Tab again, and type *$120*.

3. Using the navigation techniques listed above, complete the table in Paranormal Tours with this information:

Ghostly B & Bs, U.S.	*$480*	*$230*
Ghostly B & Bs, Europe	*$798*	*$360*
Bermuda Triangle	*$566*	*$345*

   Don't worry about bad word breaks for now. We'll fix them later in the chapter.

4. So that you can see all the data, move the table and drag the handles around the table's frame to enlarge it, like this:

From now on, size the table as needed to see its contents.

← Moving around in a table

Table math

The Formula command on Word's Table menu allows you to perform mathematical calculations on the data in your tables. For the Formula command to work, each cell in the table is assigned an address consisting of the cell's column letter and row number. The first cell is A1, the cell below A1 is A2, the cell to the right of A1 is B1, and so on. To enter a formula, click an insertion point in the cell where you want the results to appear, and then choose Formula from the Table menu. Word displays the Formula dialog box, in which you enter the formula you want to use in your calculation. If you click an insertion point in a cell below a column of numbers, choose the Formula command, and click OK in the Formula dialog box, Word uses the default formula =SUM(ABOVE) and totals the numbers in the column. To total the numbers in a row, change the formula to =SUM(RIGHT) or =SUM(LEFT), depending on the location of the insertion point. To use a function other than SUM, delete all but the equal sign in the Formula edit box, select a function from the Paste Function drop-down list, and enter the appropriate cells or cell range between the function's parentheses. (When you enter two or more cells, the cells must be separated with a comma, as in A1,D1. When you enter a cell range, the cells must be separated with a colon, as in A1:D1.)

5. To save the table, click anywhere outside the table, and then in PowerPoint, click the Save button on the Standard toolbar. (We'll make the table easier to read later.)

Inserting and Deleting Columns and Rows

The Insert and Delete commands at the top of Word's Table menu change to reflect whatever table component is currently selected. If a column is selected, we see the Insert Columns and Delete Columns commands at the top of Word's Table menu. If a row is selected, we see the Insert Rows and Delete Rows commands. If a cell is selected, the commands change to Insert Cells and Delete Cells (see the adjacent tip).

Let's insert a new column to the left of the Transport column in the sample table:

1. Double-click the table in PowerPoint to display it in Word, click any cell in the Transport column, and choose Select Column from Word's Table menu.

2. Choose Insert Columns from Word's Table menu or click the Insert Columns button on Word's Standard toolbar.

3. In the first cell of the new column, type *Hotel* as the column heading. Then fill in the remaining cells of the column with the information listed below:

$475
$695
$1,350
$1,029

Now insert a new row at the top of the table:

1. Click any cell in the first row and choose Select Row from Word's Table menu.

2. Choose Insert Rows from Word's Table menu or click the Insert Rows button on Word's Standard toolbar.

3. In the first cell of the new row, type *Paranormal Tours*.

Deleting rows and columns is as simple as inserting them. Follow these steps:

More about selecting, inserting, and deleting

Before you can insert or delete a column or row, you must make a selection so that Word knows where you want the insertion or deletion to take place. To select a column, drag through the cells of the column, or click any cell in the column and choose Select Column from Word's Table menu. To select a row, drag through the cells of the row (be sure to include the end-of-row marker), or click any cell in the row and choose Select Row from Word's Table menu. To quickly select a column in a table, point to the top of the column, and when the mouse pointer changes to a down arrow, click the left mouse button. To quickly select a row, point to the left end of the row, and when the mouse pointer changes to a right-pointing arrow, double-click to select the entire row, including the end-of-row marker. If you select multiple columns or rows before choosing the Insert or Delete command, Word inserts or deletes that many columns or rows. When you select a cell or cells in a table without selecting an entire column or row, the commands at the top of Word's Table menu become Insert Cells and Delete Cells. After choosing one of these commands, you can specify how the remaining cells should move after the insertion or deletion and whether an entire row or column should be inserted or deleted.

1. Select the last column in the table.

2. Choose Delete Columns from the Table menu.

Deleting columns

Adjusting Column Width and Row Height

The fastest ways to adjust column widths and row heights in a table are to move the gridlines between the columns and rows or to move the column and row markers on the rulers. For example, to decrease the width of a column, we can drag the column's right gridline to the left. Or, to increase the height of a row, we can drag the marker that aligns with the bottom of the row downward on the vertical ruler. Let's adjust the widths of the columns in the sample table right now:

1. Choose Ruler from Word's View menu to turn on the horizontal and vertical rulers. The rulers run along the top and left side of the table, and a tab alignment button, currently displaying the symbol for left-aligned tabs, sits at the intersection of the rulers. You can change the tab-alignment setting from left to center to right to decimal by simply clicking this button.

2. Point to the Tour column's right gridline. When the pointer changes to a double bar with arrows, hold down the left mouse button and drag to the 3½-inch position on the horizontal ruler.

3. Repeat step 2, moving the Airfare column's right gridline to the 5-inch position on the horizontal ruler, the Hotel column's right gridline to the 6½-inch position, and the Transport column's right gridline to the 8½-inch position.

4. Choose Ruler from the View menu to turn off the rulers.

Merging and Splitting Cells

To include headings that span more than one column, we can convert two or more cells to one large cell. To create a heading for the sample table, let's merge the cells in the first row:

1. Select all four cells in the first row of the table.

2. Choose Merge Cells from Word's Table menu. The result is shown on the next page.

More precise column and row adjustment

If you want a more precise way to adjust column widths and row heights (or if you want to change the widths and heights of multiple columns and rows simultaneously), make your selection and then choose Cell Height And Width from Word's Table menu. When the Cell Height And Width dialog box appears, enter the desired column width on the Column tab or the desired row height on the Row tab and click OK. (If you want to adjust the previous or next row/column, click the corresponding button in the dialog box.) You can also change other settings, such as the space between columns or the alignment of rows, in the Cell Height And Width dialog box.

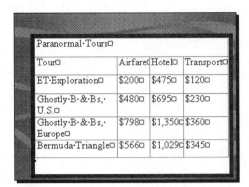

If you choose Merge Cells by mistake, you can click the Undo button to return the merged cells to their original state. If you decide later that you don't want the cells to be merged, you can choose Split Cells from Word's Table menu. Word then displays the Split Cells dialog box, in which you specify the number of columns you want to split the selected cell into.

Splitting merged cells

Formatting a Table

In addition to formatting the table's data, you can also format the table's structure, adding borders and shading for instance. In this section, we'll try our hands at both types of formatting.

Formatting a Table's Data

Because PowerPoint and Word are so closely related, the techniques for formatting data in Word are very similar to those in PowerPoint. In fact, the Formatting toolbars of both programs share many of the same buttons. As with Power-Point, we can also use commands on Word's Format and object menus to format the table's data. Follow these steps to format the data in the sample table:

Table autoformats

An easy way to apply formatting to a table is to use Word's table autoformats. Click an insertion point anywhere in the table and choose Table AutoFormat from the Table menu or click the Table AutoFormat button on the Tables And Borders toolbar (see the tip on page 86). Word displays the Table AutoFormat dialog box, where you can choose from a variety of table styles. Click an option in the Formats list to see a sample in the Preview box. Then modify the style using the options in the sections below. When you click OK to complete the changes, you instantly have a great-looking table.

1. With the table on Slide 6 displayed in Word, select the table heading in the first row by triple-clicking it, and then click the Center button on Word's Formatting toolbar.

2. Next choose Font from Word's Format menu, and on the Font tab of the Font dialog box, select Bold in the Font Style list, select 36 in the Size list, and then click OK.

3. Select all the data below the table heading, including the four column headings.

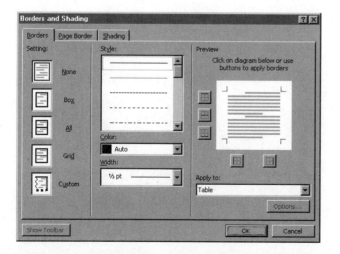

The Font Color button

4. Click the arrow to the right of the Font Color button on the Formatting toolbar and select Yellow from the drop-down palette. The data in the table will now be more legible against the dark background of the slide.

5. Next, select the Airfare, Hotel, and Transport column headings and the data below them, and click the Center button on the Formatting toolbar. Click anywhere in the table to deselect the columns. The results are shown below:

Paranormal·Tours□

Tour□	Airfare□	Hotel□	Transport□
ET·Exploration□	$200□	$475□	$120□
Ghostly·B·&·Bs,·U.S.□	$480□	$695□	$230□
Ghostly·B·&·Bs,·Europe□	$798□	$1,350□	$360□
Bermuda·Triangle□	$566□	$1,029□	$345□

Formatting a Table's Structure

If we want to dress up a table or call attention to specific information, we can add borders and/or shading using the Borders And Shading command on Word's Format menu. Try this:

1. With the slide's table displayed in Word and the insertion point located anywhere in the table, choose Borders And Shading from Word's Format menu to display this dialog box:

Moving and copying in tables

The fastest way to move a column, row, or cell in a table is to select it and drag it to its location. Hold down the Ctrl key as you drag to copy, rather than move, the column, row, or cell. (To move or copy multiple columns, rows, or cells, select them all before you drag.) You can also use the Cut, Copy, and Paste buttons on Word's Standard toolbar or the Cut, Copy, and Paste commands on Word's Edit and object menus. When moving or copying a row, you must select the entire row, including the end-of-row marker; otherwise, the contents of the destination row will be overwritten by the contents of the moved or copied row. End-of-cell markers also play an important part in determining how the contents of cells are moved or copied. If you include the end-of-cell marker in your selection, the contents of the moved or copied cell overwrite the contents of the destination cell. If you don't include the end-of-cell marker, the contents of the moved or copied cell are added to the contents of the destination cell.

Adding a border and gridlines →

2. In the Setting section, select Grid to add a border and gridlines to the table. (To add only a border, select the Box option.)

3. Change the Color setting to Yellow and the Width setting to 3 pt, and then click OK.

Adding shading →

4. Next, select the first row of the table (the row containing the table heading), right-click, and choose Borders And Shading from the object menu.

5. Click the Shading tab and click the Gray-25% box (the middle option in the second row). Then change the Color setting to Yellow and click OK.

6. Click anywhere outside the table to return to PowerPoint, and if necessary, adjust the table's position and size (see the tip below). Here's what the finished product looks like:

Having completed Part One of this Quick Course, you are now equipped to produce simple presentations that will meet most of your needs. In Part Two, we explore techniques for creating more complex presentations.

The Tables And Borders toolbar

To quickly access many useful table formatting features, display the Tables And Borders toolbar by clicking the Tables And Borders button on Word's Standard toolbar. To turn off the toolbar, simply click the button again.

Moving and sizing tables

You can use the mouse to change the location and size of a table on a slide. To move a table, first select it. Then point anywhere inside the table (in PowerPoint) or point to the table's frame (in Word) and drag the table to the desired location on the slide. To resize a table, drag its handles. (If you drag one of the corner handles, you can change the height and width of the table proportionally.)

TWO

BUILDING PROFICIENCY

In Part Two, we build on the techniques you learned in Part One to create even more sophisticated presentations. After completing these chapters, you will be able to create complex presentations that will dazzle your audience. In Chapter 4, you learn how to spruce up your presentations by adding clip art, graphics, fancy text effects, and drawing objects. In Chapter 5, we show you how to create a custom template using PowerPoint's masters feature and then apply it to an existing presentation. In Chapter 6, we wrap up the book with a more in-depth discussion of running electronic slide shows, including adding special effects.

More Fancy Effects

4

Here, we explore other ways to spruce up the slides of your presentations by adding clip art from the Microsoft Clip Gallery, importing graphics from other sources, using WordArt, and using the Power-Point drawing tools.

On Slide 8 of Paranormal Tours, we added a graphic from the Clip Gallery and changed its size, position, and color. On Slide 2, we added another graphic, cropped it, and then moved it to the background. We imported a graphic created in another program on Slide 5. And finally, we used WordArt and the drawing tools to spruce up the title of Slide 1.

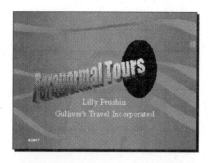

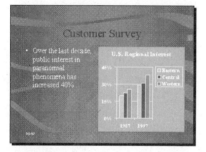

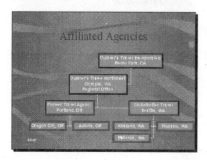

I n Part One, we allowed PowerPoint's design templates to provide graphic enhancements for our presentations. This chapter focuses on other ways to graphically enrich our slides. Even if we are not artistic, PowerPoint's Clip Gallery and drawing tools can make us look like we are. And we can also add extra flourishes with fancy text created with the WordArt feature.

The Clip Gallery

As you'll see, we can use the pictures in the Clip Gallery to dress up our slides, and with hundreds of pictures to choose from, the Clip Gallery has a picture to fit just about any need. First we show you how to add clip art graphics to slides and how to size and manipulate the graphics. We also discuss importing graphics from other sources into a PowerPoint presentation. Then we show you how to create fancy type effects using WordArt. Finally, we introduce PowerPoint's drawing tools and give some pointers for creating original graphics. If we can't find the right picture in the Clip Gallery, or if we're really creative, we can use these tools to produce our own masterpieces, which we can then add to our presentation's slides.

When PowerPoint was installed on your computer, not all of the available graphics files were copied to your hard disk. Several other files can be viewed and imported into a presentation from PowerPoint's installation disk. In our examples, we use a couple of these graphics. If you do not have Power-Point's installation disk, substitute any of the graphics that are available to you.

Adding Clip Art to Slides

We can add clip art to existing slides or select the clip art autolayouts in the New Slide dialog box to create brand new slides with clip art placeholders. Using the Paranormal Tours presentation we worked with in Chapters 1 and 3, we'll show you how to add clip art to an existing slide. (For information about creating new slides with clip art, see the tip on the facing page.) Follow these steps:

1. Start PowerPoint, open Paranormal Tours, and display Slide 8 of Paranormal Tours in slide view.

2. If it's available, insert PowerPoint's installation disk, and then click the Insert Clip Art button on the Standard toolbar or choose Picture and then Clip Art from the Insert menu. (If PowerPoint reminds you that more clip art is available on the installation disk and you don't have the disk, simply click OK.) PowerPoint then displays this dialog box:

The Insert Clip Art button

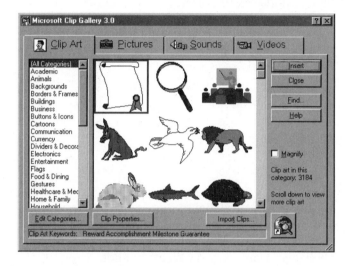

3. With (All Categories) selected in the Categories list on the left, scroll through the graphics shown in the box on the right to see what's available.

4. Select the Travel category, scroll the graphics in the box on the right, and select the first black and white globe in the twelfth row.

5. Click Insert to add the graphic to Slide 8. (You can also simply double-click the graphic.) Here are the results:

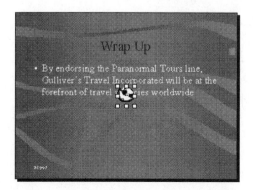

New clip art slides

If you want to create a brand new clip art slide, rather than add a clip art graphic to an existing slide, simply click the New Slide button on the Standard toolbar and select one of the clip art autolayouts in the New Slide dialog box.

6. Save the presentation. (As usual, we won't tell you to save from now on, but you should remember to save often.)

Sizing and Positioning Clip Art

Like other objects in PowerPoint, we can easily resize and relocate clip art graphics on a slide. Follow these steps to change the size and location of the globe graphic:

1. If the globe graphic is not currently selected (surrounded by handles), click it once to select it.

Sizing graphics → 2. Point to one of the graphic's bottom corner handles, and when the pointer changes to a double-headed arrow, hold down the left mouse button and drag downward until the graphic has about tripled in size.

Moving graphics → 3. Next, point anywhere inside the graphic, hold down the left mouse button, and drag downward and to the right until the graphic no longer obscures the text of the bulleted item and sits in the bottom right corner of the slide.

4. Click outside the graphic to deselect it. Slide 8 now looks something like the one shown here:

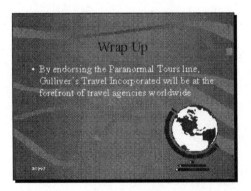

Changing Clip Art Colors

We aren't restricted to the predefined set of colors on a clip art graphic. We can use the options in the Recolor Picture dialog box to change any of the graphic's colors. Let's try recoloring the globe graphic now:

1. Select the graphic, and if necessary, display the Picture toolbar by right-clicking the graphic and choosing Show Picture Toolbar from the object menu. If the toolbar is in the way, dock it at the bottom of the screen by double-clicking its title bar.

Displaying the Picture toolbar

2. With the graphic selected, click the Recolor Picture button on the Picture toolbar to display this dialog box:

The Recolor Picture button

By default, the Fills option is selected in the Change section of the dialog box, and you can change only the background or fill colors. To change any of the clip art graphic's colors, you would select the Colors option.

3. Select both check boxes in the Original section, open one of the adjacent drop-down color palettes in the New section, and select a different color, keeping an eye on the preview box to the right to see how your selections affect the graphic.

Selecting a new color

By default, the drop-down palette presents you with the eight colors of the current color scheme. If you want to use a different color, you can click the More Colors option to display the Colors dialog box, and then select from the Colors palette or click the Custom tab to create a custom color; see page 116 for more information. If you use the color scheme offered, however, you're assured that your selection will coordinate with the other colors on the slide, and if you change the color scheme of the slide, the colors of the graphic will change accordingly.

4. When you achieve the desired effect, click OK. (We left the top box white and changed the black sections of the globe to yellow so that the graphic will show up better on the slide.)

Replacing clip art

If you change your mind about a clip art graphic you have added to a presentation, you can easily replace it. Simply double-click the graphic to open the Microsoft Clip Gallery dialog box and then select a different graphic.

Searching for Clip Art

When you first opened the Clip Gallery dialog box, you might have noticed the Find button. Rather than scroll through the hundreds of graphics in the Gallery, we can click the Find button and use the options in the Find Clip dialog box to locate a specific clip art graphic. Let's find an airplane graphic on the installation disk and insert it on Slide 2 of Paranormal Tours by following the steps below. (Again, substitute a different graphic if you don't have the installation disk.)

1. Move to Slide 2 of the Paranormal Tours presentation.

2. Click the Insert Clip Art button on the Standard toolbar, and when the Clip Gallery dialog box appears, click the Find button to display this Find Clip dialog box:

Microsoft's Clip Gallery Web page

You can click a button at the bottom of the Microsoft Clip Gallery dialog box to easily access additional clips available on Microsoft's Web site. If you use PowerPoint as part of Office 97 and are connected to the Internet, you can click the button with the globe on it and then click OK in the message box that appears. PowerPoint then connects you to the Internet and takes you to a Clip Gallery page on Microsoft's Web site. Follow the instructions on the page to search for and download a clip art graphic. (When you download a graphic from the Clip Gallery Web page, it is automatically added to the Clip Gallery under a (Downloaded Clips) category and to any other applicable categories.)

This dialog box gives you several options. Clip Gallery stores its items with a few descriptive terms attached, so you can enter a word in the Keywords edit box to find relevant graphics. If you know part or all of the clip art file's name, you can focus your search by entering that information in the File Name Containing edit box. And as graphics files can be saved in a variety of formats, you can search for graphics of a specific format by selecting a file type from the Clip Type drop-down list.

3. With the contents of the Keywords edit box highlighted, type *plane* and click Find Now to display the results shown at the top of the facing page.

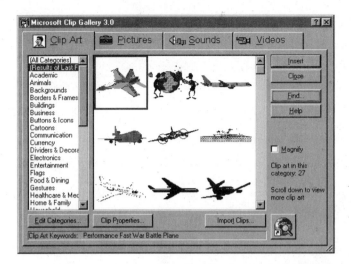

As you can see, any graphic with *plane* included in one of its keywords is displayed in the Gallery. (For example, any graphics with the keyword *planet* are also included.)

4. Double-click the third plane graphic in the sixth row to insert it on Slide 2. Don't worry if the graphic obscures the bulleted text; we'll fix that later.

If the results of a search don't identify a graphic we can use, we can always return to the Find Clip dialog box and enter a different word in the Keywords edit box or use one of the other Find options.

Cropping Clip Art

If we don't want to use all of a graphic, we can cut away the parts we don't want by *cropping* the graphic. (A cropped graphic can easily be restored to its original condition by clicking the Reset Picture button on the Picture toolbar.) In this section, we show you how to crop the plane graphic. But before we do, let's resize it:

1. With Slide 2 displayed in slide view and the graphic selected, drag one of the corner handles until the graphic has approximately tripled in size.

Adding borders to graphics

To add a border to any graphic object, select the object, and click the Format Picture button on the Picture toolbar. On the Colors And Lines tab, first change the Color setting in the Line section to the desired color, select a style and weight for the border, and then click OK.

The Crop button

2. Click the Crop button on the Picture toolbar to activate the cropping tool.

3. Place the cropping tool over the middle left handle of the graphic and drag to the right until about a quarter of the plane is cut off, like this:

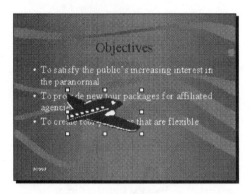

4. Click the Crop button again to deactivate the cropping tool.

5. Drag the plane graphic toward the bottom left corner of the slide as shown below. (Make sure the graphic partially obscures the text so that you can follow along in the next section.)

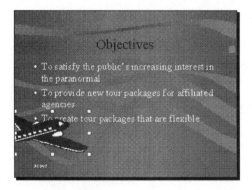

AutoClipArt

If you need help selecting appropriate clip art graphics for your presentation, you can use the AutoClipArt command. When you choose this command from the Tools menu, PowerPoint tries to match keywords from the presentation to appropriate graphics from the Clip Gallery. Select a keyword from the drop-down list in the AutoClipArt dialog box and then click the View Clip Art button. PowerPoint opens the Microsoft Clip Gallery dialog box, where it displays graphic suggestions (if any). You can then select a graphic and click Insert.

Adding Clip Art to the Background

We can add a clip art graphic to the background of one or all slides in a presentation. We'll show you how to do the former in a moment. To do the latter, we must insert the clip art graphic on the presentation's slide master and then choose Order and then Send To Back from the Draw menu. (For more information, see page 118.) Follow these steps to add the plane graphic to the background of just Slide 2 and then do a little recoloring:

1. If the Drawing toolbar isn't displayed, activate it.

2. With the graphic on Slide 2 selected, click the Draw button on the Drawing toolbar to display a menu of options. Choose Order and then Send To Back. The text of the slide now overlays the graphic.

3. To make the text of the last bulleted item more legible, click the Recolor Picture button on the Picture toolbar to display its dialog box.

4. Click the black Original check box, click the arrow to the right of the adjacent New box, then select the seventh of the eight color-scheme colors, and click OK. Here's what Slide 2 looks like now:

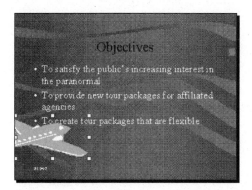

Importing Graphics from Other Sources

For those times when we want to use a graphic from another application, PowerPoint can import a multitude of graphics file formats, as long as we have installed the proper graphics filters. (If Microsoft Word or Microsoft Excel is installed on your computer, PowerPoint can share the filters that came with those programs.) Turn the page to see a list of the graphics file formats you can import into PowerPoint presentations.

Graphics file formats

Graphics file format	Extension
AutoCAD Format 2-D	.DXF
Computer Graphics Metafile	.CGM
CorelDRAW	.CDR
Encapsulated PostScript	.EPS
Enhanced Metafile	.EMF
Graphics Interchange Format	.GIF
Joint Photographics Experts Group	.JPG
Kodak Photo CD	.PCD
Macintosh PICT	.PCT
Micrografx Designer/Draw	.DRW
PC Paintbrush	.PCX
Portable Network Graphics	.PNG
Tagged Image File Format	.TIF
Targa	.TGA
Windows Bitmap	.BMP
Windows Metafile	.WMF
WordPerfect Graphics	.WPG

The procedure for importing graphics into PowerPoint is a snap. To demonstrate just how easy it is to pull a graphic in from another source, we used the Windows 95 Paint program to create a simple graphic called Ufo.bmp, which we will insert on Slide 5 of Paranormal Tours. If you have a graphics file handy (any graphics file will do), you can follow along now:

1. In slide view, move to Slide 5, and from the Insert menu, choose Picture and then choose From File to display the Insert Picture dialog box shown below. (If the Picture toolbar is displayed, you can click the Insert Picture From File button.)

The Insert Picture From File button

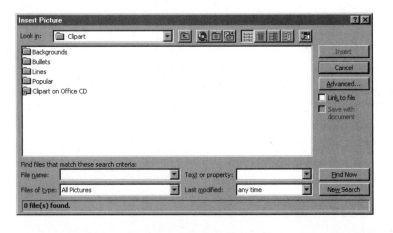

Importing graphics from the Web

If you have access to the Internet, you can import the graphics you download from Web sites into your presentations. (However, be sure anything you download is virus-free before you use it.)

2. Move to the folder where the graphics file is located. (Make sure the correct file type appears in the Files Of Type box. If it doesn't, select the type you need from the drop-down list.)

3. Double-click the graphics file (UFO, in our case) in the list box to insert the graphic on the current slide, as shown here:

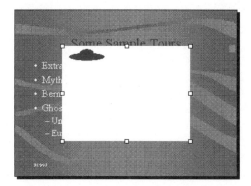

4. Use the cropping tool to cut away any parts of the graphic you don't want, and then drag the graphic to the right of the first bulleted item.

5. Click the Set Transparent Color button on the Picture toolbar, and click the background of the graphic so that the slide background shows through. Here are the results:

The Set Transparent Color button

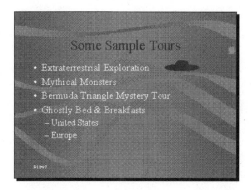

You can use the techniques described earlier to resize an imported graphic or to add it to the slide's background. You can also recolor some types of imported graphics.

Scanned images

Like graphics files, you can easily import scanned images into your PowerPoint presentations. In slide view, first display the slide where you want to place the image and then choose Picture and From File from the Insert menu. In the Insert Picture dialog box, select the file containing the scanned image and click OK. You can then crop, move, and resize the image like any other imported graphic. (If you don't have a scanner at your disposal, you can always take photographs or other images to a copy center or photo lab to have them scanned.)

Adding Graphics to the Clip Gallery

If we want graphics from other applications to be as readily available as the clip art that came with PowerPoint, we can add the graphics to the Clip Gallery. Just follow the steps below. (Again, we'll use Ufo.bmp as an example.)

1. Click the Insert Clip Art button on the Standard toolbar to open the Clip Gallery dialog box, and then click the Import Clips button to display this dialog box:

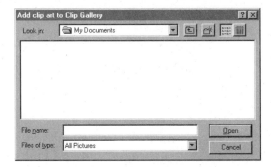

2. If necessary, select the type of graphic file you want to add from the Files Of Type drop-down list (Windows Bitmaps, in our case) and then navigate to the folder where the file is located.

3. Double-click the name of the graphic file. PowerPoint imports the file and then displays the Clip Properties dialog box, where a picture of the graphic appears in the top right corner:

More Clip Gallery options

In addition to the Import Clips button in the Clip Gallery dialog box, you'll find two other buttons: Clip Properties and Edit Categories. You can use the Clip Properties button to change the description and/or category of the selected graphic. You can use the Edit Categories button to add, rename, or delete a category. (If a graphic is listed only in a category you want to delete, the graphic will be deleted from the Clip Gallery as well.)

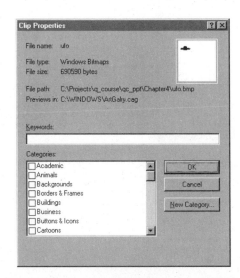

4. Type some words in the Keywords edit box. (We entered *Flying Saucers, UFO,* and *Extraterrestrial,* separating the words with commas.)

5. Select a category name in the Categories list or click the New Category button and enter a new name. (We entered the name *Paranormal.*) Then click OK.

6. Click the Pictures tab to display the dialog box shown below. (Yours will look different if you don't have the installation disk loaded.)

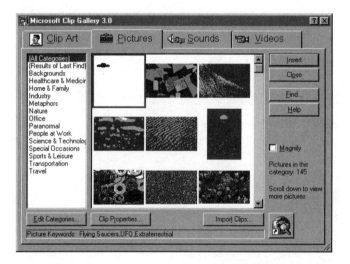

If your graphic is large, it may take a few minutes for PowerPoint to add it to the Clip Gallery.

7. Click Close to exit the Gallery.

Now, whenever we want to insert the UFO graphic, we can simply click the Insert Clip Art button and select the graphic from the Pictures tab of the Microsoft Clip Gallery.

Using WordArt for Fancy Type Effects

The Paranormal Tours presentation is quite "presentable" as it is, except that the title slide needs to grab more attention. In earlier chapters, you learned how to create an impact by changing the font and size of the text on a slide. In this chapter, we'll introduce you to WordArt, which we can use to mold

Adding sounds and videos to slides

Included in the Microsoft Clip Gallery dialog box are the Sounds and Videos tabs. If you have the necessary hardware and have inserted the installation disk, you can click one of these tabs to view several multimedia options. To make a selection, simply double-click the file you want to insert on the active slide. Any sounds you insert will be marked by a speaker icon, which can be resized and moved. To test the sound in slide view, double-click the speaker icon. To play the sound during an on-screen presentation, click the speaker icon once. For videos, PowerPoint places an image on the slide, where it can be moved and resized. To show the video, follow the same procedure for playing a sound.

text into various shapes to fit the mood of the presentation or to flow around other elements on a slide. (In previous versions of PowerPoint, WordArt was a separate program, but now this capability is part of PowerPoint.)

Follow these steps to jazz up the title slide of the Paranormal Tours presentation:

1. Display the title slide of Paranormal Tours, click the title area, and then press the F2 key to select the area rather than the title itself.

2. Press the Delete key twice to remove the title and the area.

The Insert WordArt button

3. Click the Insert WordArt button on the Drawing toolbar to display this WordArt Gallery dialog box:

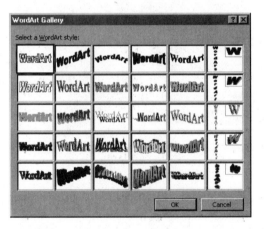

More WordArt options

The WordArt toolbar comes with a variety of buttons. To edit the WordArt text or change its font or size, click the WordArt Edit Text button. To change the style, click the WordArt Gallery button to redisplay its dialog box. To change the color, size, or position, click the Format WordArt button. You can use the remaining buttons to alter the shape, rotation, letter height, orientation, alignment, and character spacing of the WordArt object. You can also change the object's shape by dragging its diamond-shaped *adjustment handle* in any direction. As you drag the handle, a dotted outline shows the approximate shape the object will assume when you release the mouse button.

4. Click the fourth option in the last row and click OK to display this dialog box:

5. Type *Paranormal Tours* and click OK to embed a WordArt object in the shape we chose in the slide and to display the WordArt toolbar, as shown here:

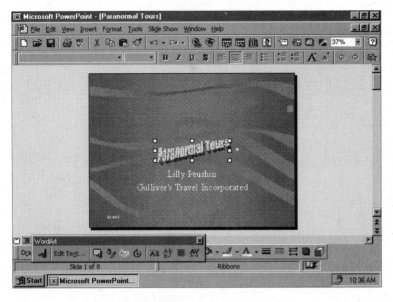

Obviously, a few adjustments are in order. In addition to changing the position and size of the new title text, we need to change its color. Here goes:

1. First, dock the WordArt toolbar at the bottom of the window by double-clicking its title bar.

2. Click the Format WordArt button on the WordArt toolbar to display the dialog box shown here:

The Format WordArt button

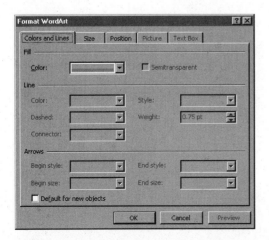

Changing the color of
WordArt text

→ 3. Click the arrow to the right of the Color box and select the
Yellow box in the next to last row. Click the Color box's arrow
again and click Fill Effects to display this dialog box:

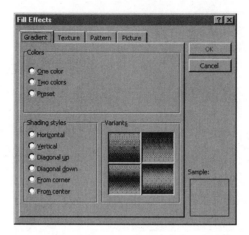

4. Click the One Color option in the Colors section of the
Gradient tab, and then click OK twice. (See the tip on page
65 for more information about fill effects.) Now the color of
the text matches the color scheme of the rest of the slides in
the Paranormal Tours presentation.

Repositioning and resizing
WordArt text

→ 5. Using the mouse and the handles, reposition and resize the
title text until it looks something like this:

Editing WordArt objects

If you want to make changes to a
WordArt object after you have
embedded it in a slide, double-
click the object to display the
WordArt toolbar as well as the
Edit WordArt Text dialog box.
You can then edit the text or use
toolbar buttons to make adjustments. When you're finished,
click outside the WordArt frame
to return to PowerPoint.

6. Click anywhere outside the WordArt object to deselect it.

Using PowerPoint's Drawing Tools

So far we have only used a few of the buttons on the Drawing toolbar. In this section, we'll briefly discuss some of the tools that are used to draw graphic objects on slides. A detailed discussion of all the drawing tools is beyond the scope of this book, so we'll show you a simple example and then leave you to explore on your own. Before we start drawing, let's set up the screen like this:

1. With Slide 1 displayed in slide view, choose Ruler from the View menu to display the rulers.

Displaying rulers

2. Choose Guides from the View menu to display horizontal and vertical lines that help you position your drawings. Your screen now looks like this:

Displaying guides

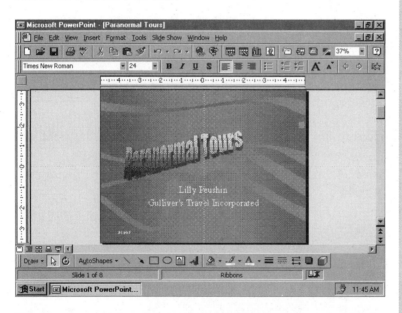

We can drag each guide to position it where we need it. As we drag, the guide's distance from the corresponding ruler's zero mark—zero is the center—is displayed so that we can use the guide to precisely position objects on the slide. For example, to position a rectangle so that its top and bottom edges are, respectively, exactly 1 inch above and 2 inches

AutoShapes

You can use the Drawing toolbar's AutoShapes button to add more complex shapes to your slides. For example, you can add a star by clicking the AutoShapes button, choosing Stars And Banners from the menu, and selecting the shape you want from the palette of options. Then position the mouse pointer on the slide, hold down the left mouse button, and drag the shape into place. You can resize the shape by dragging its handles, or reposition it by dragging it to a new location. If the autoshape has a diamond-shaped adjustment handle, you can drag the handle to adjust the shape's most prominent characteristic. (For example, you can change the angle of an isosceles triangle by dragging its adjustment handle.) To quickly replace an autoshape, select the shape, click the Draw button on the Drawing toolbar, choose Change AutoShape, and select a different shape from the drop-down palette of options.

below a slide's center, we would drag the horizontal guide to the 1-inch mark above the zero on the vertical ruler and draw the rectangle from the guide to approximately the 2-inch mark below the zero on the vertical ruler. Then we would drag the horizontal guide to the 2-inch mark and align the bottom edge of the rectangle with the guide. To add guides, we hold down the Ctrl key as we grab a displayed guide. The original guide remains stationary as we drag a new guide. To place the new guide, release the mouse button and then release the Ctrl key. To remove a guide, we can simply drag it off the slide.

Adding and removing guides

We can draw a number of basic shapes, including lines, rectangles, and squares, using the tools on the Drawing toolbar. To get a feel for drawing shapes and working with the Drawing toolbar, let's create a "black hole" on the title slide of the Paranormal Tours presentation:

The Oval button

1. With Slide 1 displayed in slide view, click the Oval button on the Drawing toolbar.

2. Position the crosshair pointer at the right end of the *Paranormal Tours* title.

3. Hold down the left mouse button and drag to the right and down, until the oval is about 3 inches high and 1½ inches wide. (Remember to use the guides.) The oval should obscure the last few letters of the title text, like this:

Additional shapes

By holding down the Ctrl and Shift keys while you use certain Drawing toolbar buttons, you can draw other shapes. For example, if you hold down Ctrl and Shift while using the Oval button, you can draw a circle.

4. With the oval selected (surrounded by handles), click the arrow to the right of the Fill Color button on the Drawing toolbar, and select the third color-scheme color.

The Fill Color button

The Line Color button

5. Next click the arrow to the right of the Line Color button on the Drawing toolbar and select No Line from the top of the palette to remove the border surrounding the oval.

6. Click the Draw button and then choose Order and Send To Back. The oval no longer obscures the title text.

7. Use the mouse (and the guides) to reposition the oval so that it's centered over the last three letters of the title.

8. Click anywhere outside the oval to deselect it. Then turn off the rulers and the guides to see these results:

With all the clip art supplied by PowerPoint, as well as graphics from other applications, WordArt, and PowerPoint's drawing tools, you shouldn't have any trouble adding a dash of excitement to your presentations. Just remember to keep it simple; otherwise, your audience might start paying more attention to your artwork than to the content of your presentation.

Rotating, flipping, and aligning objects

You can use the Free Rotate button on the Drawing toolbar or the Free Rotate command on the Rotate Or Flip submenu of the Draw menu to rotate an object about its center. Simply select the object, click the toolbar button or choose the command, point to one of the object's corner handles, and drag to the left or right. If you want to rotate an object exactly 90 degrees to the left or right, select the object and then choose the appropriate command from the Rotate Or Flip submenu of the Draw menu. To flip objects horizontally or vertically, select the object and choose the equivalent command from the Rotate Or Flip submenu. Finally, you can align several objects on a slide in various ways by selecting the objects (hold down the Shift key as you click each object), choosing Align Or Distribute from the Draw menu, and then choosing one of the commands from the submenu.

Creating a Custom Template

We cover how to design and customize your own template by using PowerPoint's masters. As we create the template, we change the font, add a graphic to the background, and change the color scheme. Then we apply the custom template to an existing presentation.

We created our own design template by changing the font, background, and bullet character of a slide master. We also added a footer and slide number to the template and changed its color scheme. Then we applied the new template to the Sample Tours presentation.

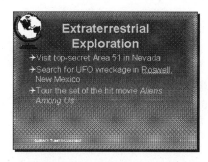

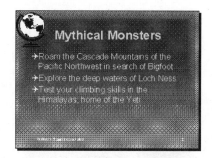

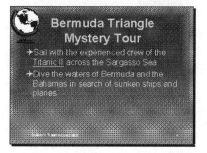

PowerPoint provides a wide variety of design templates to choose from, but you might be happy to know that we aren't limited to those templates. We can create our own templates either by modifying an existing template or by designing a new one from scratch. In this chapter, we show you how to create a brand new template, with the fonts, bullet characters, color scheme, and so on, of our own choosing. Then we apply the new template to the Sample Tours presentation we built in Chapter 2, so that you can see how a custom template looks in action.

Designing a Template

Before we start a new template, we need to ask ourselves a few simple questions. For example, what kind of message or feeling do we want the template to convey? Should the template have a formal or informal look? What sort of design elements do we want to include? After we've sorted out the answers to these questions, we can begin working on the actual template design.

For the purposes of this chapter, we want to create a template that can be applied to the Sample Tours presentation. Because the presentation's topic is travel (in other words, recreation), a relaxed, less formal look is probably the best choice. We can also play off the subject of the paranormal by using colors and shading that invoke a feeling of mystery and suspense. With these decisions out of the way, follow the steps below to open a blank slide:

1. Start PowerPoint, and when the PowerPoint dialog box appears, double-click the Blank Presentation option to open the New Slide dialog box.

2. Next, double-click the Title Slide autolayout. PowerPoint displays a blank slide like the one shown at the top of the facing page.

Corporate templates

With the advent of presentation programs, which have greatly simplified the task of creating presentations, many companies no longer need special departments to handle the making of slides, overhead transparencies, and so on. Now any Tom, Dick, or Mary can put together a presentation in no time at all. As a result, many companies have established guidelines to avoid potentially embarrassing situations, such as presentations with gaudy colors or illegible fonts. To ensure the quality and consistency of every presentation, large companies are developing corporate templates that every employee can use. What's more, logos, special colors, and fonts are often included in these templates to give them a real corporate look. If you work for a company that has recently standardized on a particular presentation program, such as Power-Point, but has not yet developed its own corporate templates, you might want to create templates that all the members of your department can use.

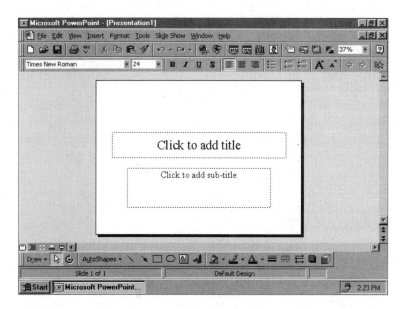

Although you're probably anxious to start creating your own template, take a moment to read the following section on masters, which are an integral part of the template design process.

Using Masters

As their name suggests, masters control the formatting of a presentation's slides. In earlier versions of PowerPoint, one master controlled all the slide types. In PowerPoint 97, the title master controls the formatting of title slides only, while the slide master controls the formatting of all other slide types. (PowerPoint 97 also includes a notes master and a handout master. See the tips on pages 112 and 113.) In this chapter, we use the slide master to create a custom template. Although we want our presentations to be attractive, we don't want the look of the slides to be more memorable than the message. One sure way to distract an audience is to vary the look of a presentation from slide to slide. By using masters as the foundation for a template, we can ensure that all the slides to which the template is applied have consistent fonts, background, and color scheme. Masters also give an easy way to make across-the-board changes to the look of our presentations, because we can, for example, change the formatting of all the slides in a presentation except the title slide by changing the formatting of the slide master.

Formatting the title master

The techniques for creating and formatting the title master are the same as those for the slide master. To display the title master, switch to master view by choosing Master and then Title Master from the View menu. To create a new title master, first switch to master view and then choose New Title Master from the Insert menu. You can then make all your formatting changes using the techniques described in this chapter.

Formatting the Slide Master

With that background discussion of template design and PowerPoint's masters out of the way, we're ready to begin creating the custom template. Because the Sample Tours presentation has no title slide, we won't bother formatting the title master. Instead, we'll work with the slide master. Bear in mind, however, that the techniques we'll discuss can also be used to format the title master (see the tip on the previous page for more information).

Changing the Font

In Chapter 2, we showed you how to change the size and style of text using the Formatting toolbar. In this section, we introduce you to the Font dialog box. While the toolbar provides quick access to different font effects, the Font dialog box offers a wider range of effects, including superscript, subscript, and embossment. Follow these steps to change the font of the slide master:

Displaying the slide master → 1. With the title slide of the blank presentation displayed on your screen, choose Master and then Slide Master from the View menu. Here's what the slide master looks like:

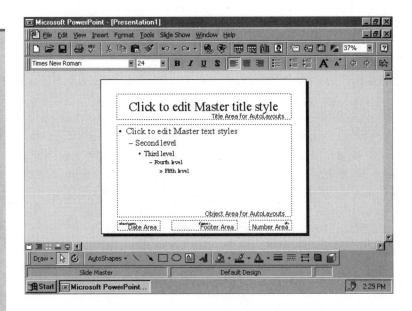

Using the notes master

If you want to create a customized look for speaker's notes, you can enlist the help of the notes master. To activate the notes master, choose Master and then Notes Master from the View menu. (You can also access the notes master by holding down the Shift key and clicking the Notes Pages View button.) You can use the notes master to add headers, footers, the date, and slide number to your speaker's notes. You can also use this master to customize the look of the bulleted items on your notes. For more information about speaker's notes, see page 26.

As you can see, the slide master is divided into several areas. We discuss each of these areas as we progress through the chapter. For now, take a moment to study the slide master and then move on to the next step.

2. Click the title area on the master and choose Font from the Format menu to display the Font dialog box:

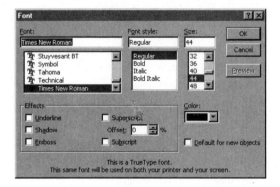

3. Select Arial in the Font list, Bold in the Font Style list, and 48 in the Size list and then click OK.

4. Next click the object area on the master and select the text of the first bulleted item.

5. Right-click the selected text, choose Font from the object menu, and when the Font dialog box appears, select Arial from the Font list and click OK.

6. Select the text of the subordinate item (remember, the Sample Tours presentation has two bullet levels) and repeat step 5. Here are the results:

Using the handout master

If you have created handouts for your presentation, you cannot view them before they are printed. However, you can get an idea of how they will look by viewing the handout master. To activate this feature, choose Master and then Handout Master from the View menu. (You can also access the handout master by holding down the Shift key and clicking the Slide Sorter View button.) When the handout master appears on your screen, the slides of your presentation are represented by boxes with dashed lines. The buttons on the Handout Master toolbar let you change the layout of the handouts to display two, three, or six slides or to display the outline of the presentation only. (To change the orientation of the slides on the handout, see the tip on page 21.) You can also use the handout master to add other elements to your handouts, such as headers, footers, and the date. To learn more about handouts, see page 28.

Saving the Template

Well, we still have quite a bit of design work to do, but before we go any further, we should save the slide master as a template to safeguard our changes. We'll store the template in the Presentation Designs folder, where PowerPoint's other templates are located. Follow these steps:

1. Choose Save As from the File menu, and when the Save As dialog box appears, click the arrow next to the Save As Type box and select Presentation Template.

2. Double-click the Presentation Designs folder in the list below the Save In box.

3. In the File Name edit box, type *Travel* as the name of the custom template, and then click Save.

As with any ordinary PowerPoint presentation, from now on we can simply click the Save button to save any changes we make to the new template. (Although we won't explicitly tell you to, you should save your work often.)

Creating a Background

If you look at the templates that ship with PowerPoint, you'll notice that all of them have colored patterns and some sort of graphic gracing their backgrounds. We can create a background with specific colors, patterns, textures, and so on, by using PowerPoint's Background command. We can also use this command to add a graphic to the background (see the tip on page 116). Let's create a background for the Travel template:

Quick font switch

If you aren't concerned with font size and you want to quickly change a specific font in a presentation, choose Replace Fonts from the Format menu. In the Replace Font dialog box, specify the font you want to replace, specify the replacement font, and then click the Replace button. The dialog box remains open so that you can make other font changes to your presentation. When you're finished, click the Close button.

1. With the slide master for the Travel template displayed, choose Background from the Format menu to display this dialog box:

As you can see, PowerPoint supplies a ready-made color scheme, as depicted in the sample slide in the Background Fill section of the dialog box. Currently, the background of the slide is white. (If you were to add a graph, its markers would have the colors shown in the sample graph.)

2. Click the arrow to the right of the blank edit box in the Background Fill section to display this drop-down list of options:

3. Change the background color by selecting the seventh of the eight boxes in the color-scheme row (lilac, in our case). The background of the sample slide instantly changes. Now click the Preview button and notice that the color of the slide master's background has changed as well. (If the Background dialog box blocks your view, you can drag its title bar.)

Changing the background color

4. Click the arrow in the Background Fill section again, select the Fill Effects option, and then click the Pattern tab to display these options:

Adding a background pattern

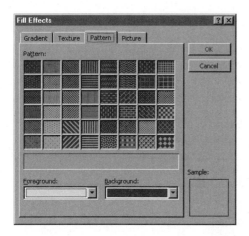

5. Select a pattern option in the Patterns section and notice the effect in the Sample box at the bottom of the dialog box.

Adding a background
texture

6. Experiment with some of the other patterns and then click the Texture tab to display these options:

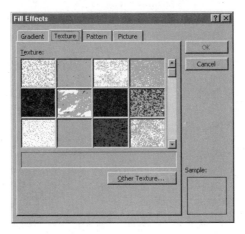

7. Experiment with some of the other texture options and then click the Cancel button.

Already you can get a feel for the range of background possibilities that PowerPoint has to offer. As you'll see if you follow these steps, you can even customize the color:

Creating a custom color

1. With the Background dialog box still open on your screen, select the More Colors option from the Background Fill drop-down list. The Colors dialog box appears, displaying the standard colors used to create the slide master's current color scheme.

2. Click the Custom tab to display these options:

Using a graphic as the background

To use a graphic as the background for slides, click the Picture tab of the Fill Effects dialog box. Then click the Select Picture button to display the Select Picture dialog box, navigate to the location of the picture file you want to use, and double-click the filename. Click OK twice to close the Select Picture and Fill Effects dialog boxes and click Apply or Apply To All to close the Background dialog box. PowerPoint then uses the graphic to fill the slide background.

3. Half hidden at the top of the Colors box is a crosshair. Point to it and drag it anywhere in the box. When you release the mouse button, PowerPoint displays the color you've selected in the New box; analyzes its red, green, and blue content, as well as its hue, saturation, and luminance; and identifies the luminance (intensity) on the vertical scale to the right of the Colors box.

4. Now point to the arrow next to the vertical luminance scale, and drag it up and down, noting the changes in the New box and in the Lum, Red, Green, and Blue boxes.

Changing color intensity

5. Take a little time to explore the Colors dialog box further. Then, when you're ready, use the arrows at the end of the three boxes below the Colors box to specify the settings for hue, saturation, and luminance shown here:

Hue	*155*
Sat(uration)	*165*
Lum(inance)	*155*

As you enter each setting, the positions of the crosshair and the vertical luminance scale arrow change, as do the settings in the Red, Green, and Blues boxes and the color in the New box.

6. Click OK to return to the Background dialog box.

Before you apply the new color to the slide master, let's include a bit of shading, just for interest:

1. Select the Fill Effects option from the Background Fill drop-down list and click the Gradient tab to display the dialog box shown earlier on page 104.

Adding shading

2. Select One Color in the Colors section and From Title in the Shading Styles section. Then double-click the second box in the Variants section.

3. Click Apply to apply the new color and shading to the slide master of the Travel template. The results are shown on the next page.

Changing hue and saturation

When you create a custom color in PowerPoint, you can change the hue and saturation of the color by simply dragging the crosshair in the Colors box. To change the hue, drag the crosshair horizontally across the Colors box. To change the saturation, drag the crosshair vertically.

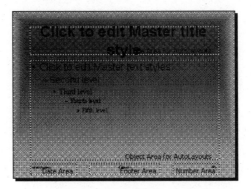

Adding a Graphic to the Background

As we mentioned earlier, we can use the Background command to make a graphic the entire background of a slide or template. If we want a graphic to occupy only part of the background, we must use the techniques discussed in Chapter 4 instead. For the Travel template, let's insert a clip art graphic from the Clip Gallery and then resize and reposition it as appropriate for the background. (We assume that you've read Chapter 4 and are familiar with the Clip Gallery. We also assume that you have the PowerPoint installation disk available. If you don't, substitute any available graphic.) Here goes:

1. With the Travel template displayed in slide master view, insert the installation disk, and click the Insert Clip Art button on the Standard toolbar.

2. When the Microsoft Clip Gallery dialog box appears, scroll the Categories list and click Travel. Then scroll the graphics in the adjacent box and double-click the globe graphic we used in Chapter 4.

3. With the graphic selected, drag its corner handles outward until it is about 1.5 inches in height and width (you can display the rulers and use them as a guide). Then point anywhere inside the graphic and drag it to the top left corner of the slide master.

4. With the graphic still selected, click the Draw button on the Drawing toolbar and choose Order and then Send To Back so that the graphic does not obscure the slide title. Now the graphic will appear "behind" any title text, as shown at the top of the facing page.

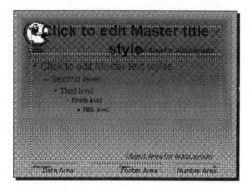

Changing the Bullet Character

Although changing the bullet character might not be as dramatic as altering the color scheme or adding a graphic, it can have an impact on the overall look of your presentation. PowerPoint offers a wide variety of bullet characters to choose from, as you'll see when you follow these steps:

1. With the Travel template open in slide master view, click an insertion point in the first bulleted item.

2. Choose Bullet from the Format menu to display the dialog box shown here:

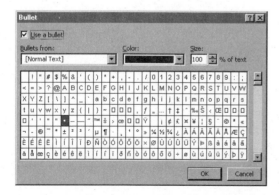

3. Click the arrow to the right of the Bullets From box and select Wingdings from the drop-down list. (If the Wingdings font is not available, select another font that contains symbols you can use as bullet characters.)

Selecting a new character

4. Select a symbol that you think would be appropriate for a bullet character. (We selected the airplane symbol in the second row of the Wingdings palette.)

5. Click OK to return to the slide master with the new character in place.

6. Click an insertion point in the second bulleted item and repeat steps 2 through 4 above. Then double-click *100* in the Size box and type *80* to reduce the size of the character a bit.

7. Click OK to return to the slide master. Here are the results:

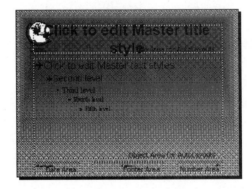

Adding a Footer and a Slide Number

At the bottom of the slide master, you may have noticed three boxes labeled Date Area, Footer Area, and Number Area. Information we enter in these boxes is added to each slide in the presentation. By default, the boxes sit at the bottom of the slide master, but we can move them to any part of the slide. Follow these steps to add a footer and a slide number:

1. Click the slide master's Footer Area box to select it. Power-Point surrounds the box with a shaded border.

2. Click the arrow to the right of the Zoom box on the Standard toolbar and select 100% from the drop-down list. Now you can see the footer area more clearly.

3. Double-click the *<footer>* placeholder and press the Delete key. (Although this placeholder won't appear on the actual slide, it will continue to show up on the slide master unless you delete it.) Then type *Gulliver's Travel Incorporated*.

Adjusting dates, footers, and slide numbers

To change the location of a date, footer, or slide number on a slide, switch to slide master view, select the Date Area, Footer Area, or Number Area box, and drag it to a new location on the slide master. You can also increase or decrease the size of any box by dragging its handles in the appropriate direction.

Adding the footer is pretty straightforward, but adding the slide number is a bit trickier. We must use the Header And Footer command on the View menu, like this:

1. Scroll the slide to the right, click the Number Area box to select it, and choose Header And Footer from the View menu. PowerPoint displays the Header And Footer dialog box:

Adding a slide number

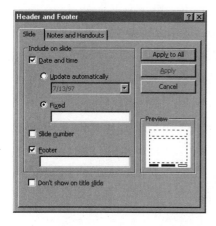

2. Select the Slide Number option and click Apply To All.

3. Now switch to slide view so that you can check the footer and slide number. (Don't worry if the text is a bit dark. We'll remedy the situation in the next section.)

Everything looks pretty good, but we should shift the footer to the bottom left corner of the slide to create balance. While we're at it, let's change the font of both the footer and the slide number to correspond with the title and bulleted text font. Follow these steps:

1. Switch to slide master view by holding down the Shift key and clicking the Slide View button.

2. Select Fit from the bottom of the Zoom drop-down list so that you can see the entire slide master.

3. Select the Date Area box and press the Delete key.

Inserting the date, time, and slide number

You can insert the date, time, and/or slide number on individual slides by displaying the slide in need of the date, time, or slide number and then choosing Header And Footer from the View menu. Select the appropriate options in the dialog box and then click Apply. The option(s) you selected appear only on the current slide. To display the date, time, and/or slide number on every slide in a presentation, click the Apply To All button in the Header And Footer dialog box.

Repositioning the footer

4. Select the Footer Area box and drag it to the left, to the position previously occupied by the Date Area box. As you drag, be careful to keep the top of the Footer Area box aligned with the top of the Number Area box. (If you have trouble positioning the box, try clicking the Draw button on the Drawing toolbar, choosing Nudge, and then selecting the appropriate direction command.)

Changing the footer and slide number font

5. With the Footer Area box still selected, drag through the footer text and choose Arial from the Font drop-down list on the Formatting toolbar. Next drag through the slide number placeholder (<#>) in the Number Area box and repeat this step for the slide number. (If you have trouble seeing the placeholders, use the Zoom drop-down list to increase the magnification.) Here's what the slide master looks like now:

Ready-made color schemes

The Standard tab of the Color Scheme dialog box provides a number of ready-made color schemes for your presentations. (The color schemes vary depending on the template that is currently in use.) To apply one of these color schemes to your presentation, simply double-click it. To apply a color scheme to the current slide only, select the scheme and then click Apply. You don't want to bombard your audience with a plethora of color, so exercise caution when you apply different color schemes to different slides (see the tip on page 125).

Changing the Color Scheme

Before we actually put our template to the test, we need to make one more significant change. As you've already seen, the color of the text makes it difficult to read against the background color we selected. Using the Font dialog box to change the text color would be tedious because we would have to work with each individual line of text. Instead, we can use the Slide Color Scheme dialog box to change all the text at once. Here's how:

1. With the Travel template displayed in slide master view, choose the Slide Color Scheme command from the Format menu, and when the Color Scheme dialog box appears, click the Custom tab to display these options:

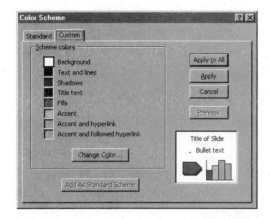

The boxes in the Scheme Colors section of the dialog box depict the colors of the various elements on the current slide. (Because we changed the background color using the Custom Background dialog box, the current background color is not reflected here.) As you'll see in a moment, you can click an element's color box and then click the Change Color button to alter all occurrences of that element. The table below describes the elements affected by the eight color boxes:

The slide elements

Color box	Affected elements
Background	Slide background.
Text And Lines	Bulleted text and text entered in a box created with the Text Box drawing tool. Also, lines and arrows drawn with the Line drawing tool and the outlines for AutoShapes and objects drawn with any of the drawing tools.
Shadows	Shadows created with the Shadow drawing tool.
Title Text	Slide titles.
Fills	Interior of AutoShapes and objects drawn with the drawing tools. Also, the first series in a graph.
Accent	Second color in graphs, organization charts, and other added elements.
Accent And Hyperlink	Third color in graphs, organization charts, and other added elements (including hyperlinks).
Accent And Followed Hyperlink	Fourth color in graphs, organization charts, and other added elements (including followed hyperlinks).

Changing the text and
line color

2. Click the Text And Lines box and then click the Change Color
   button to display this Text And Line Color dialog box:

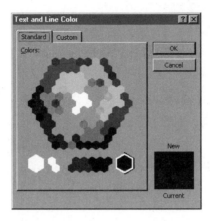

3. Select the White hexagon in the bottom left corner of the
   Standard tab (below the color palette) and click OK. When
   you return to the Color Scheme dialog box, notice that the
   Text And Lines box is now white.

Changing the title text color

4. Next click the Title Text box and click the Change Color
   button.

Designating a standard scheme

If you've developed your own
color scheme and want to save it
for future use, you'll be happy to
know that PowerPoint provides a
way to save the color scheme
with the current presentation. After you create your scheme, click
the Add As Standard Scheme
button found on the Custom tab
of the Color Scheme dialog box.
PowerPoint adds the new color
scheme to the Standard tab.
Then, whenever you open the
corresponding presentation,
your custom color scheme is
available for use. (To delete the
scheme, simply select it on the
Standard tab and click the Delete
Scheme button.)

5. When the Title Text Color dialog box appears, click the
   Custom tab to display options similar to those in the Colors
   dialog box shown earlier on page 116.

6. Drag the crosshair in the Colors box and the arrow along the
   vertical color bar until the Hue, Sat(uration), and Lum(inance)
   settings read as specified below. (Remember, you can also
   use the arrows at the end of each box to change the settings.)

Hue	*196*
Sat(uration)	*140*
Lum(inance)	*104*

7. Click OK to return to the Color Scheme dialog box, where
   the Title Text color box is now purple.

8. Finally, click the Apply button to apply the new color scheme
   to the slide master. (If you were working with the slides of an
   actual presentation, rather than a slide master, you would click

the Apply To All button to apply the new color scheme to all the slides of the presentation.)

Although we only made a couple of changes to the color scheme for the Travel template, we were careful to select colors that complemented one another. Before you start creating color schemes on your own, be sure to read the adjacent tip about the effect of color.

Applying a Custom Template

After all that work, you're probably anxious to apply your custom template to the Sample Tours presentation. Before we do, however, bear in mind the following: because we are applying the template to a set of preexisting slides, we might have to make a few minor adjustments, such as repositioning the title or object area. Usually these adjustments won't be necessary if we select a template first and then add text to our slides. Nonetheless, we'll walk you through any changes that have to be made. Let's put the custom template to the test:

1. With the Travel template open in slide master view, click the Save button and then choose Close from the File menu.

2. Open the Sample Tours presentation and click the Apply Design button on the Standard toolbar.

3. Scroll the list of templates in the Apply Design dialog box, select Travel, (note the sample in the preview box), and then click Apply. Here's what Slide 1 looks like now:

4. Save the presentation with the new template in place.

The effect of color

The colors you use in your presentations are just as important as the fonts you use. Like fonts, different colors can send different messages to your audience. For example, "cool" colors such as green, blue, and violet are associated with oceans and pastoral settings and can imply peace and tranquillity. "Warm" colors such as red, orange, and yellow, on the other hand, are associated with fire and can imply aggression and intensity. You also need to be aware of these factors when selecting colors for a presentation:

- Use cool colors, which tend to recede from the audience, as background colors. Use warm colors, which tend to advance, to call attention to specific items.

- Similarly, use bright colors to visually advance an element. Muted or darker colors will recede.

- When creating electronic slides, use a dark background. For overheads and 35mm slides, use a light background.

- Avoid placing red and green next to each other. (People who are color-blind may not be able to distinguish between them.)

- Use color to highlight data. For example, format positive numbers in blue and negative numbers in red.

- Resist temptation. Too many colors together can distract your audience. Instead, select color to focus attention on a few key areas.

Fine-Tuning

As we mentioned earlier, you may have to make a few adjustments to the Sample Tours presentation after the new template is applied. Take a moment now to scroll through the slides of the presentation. Notice anything wrong? Well, for starters, the slide number is missing from our slides. If your presentation is also lacking this information, follow these steps:

Displaying the slide numbers →

1. With Slide 1 of Sample Tours displayed in slide view, choose Header And Footer from the View menu.

2. When the Header And Footer dialog box appears, select the Slide Number option and click Apply To All.

Now scroll through the slides again to check the placement of titles, bulleted text, footers, and so on. It looks like the bulleted text of Slide 3 could use a little adjusting. Let's reposition the object area so that the last bulleted item doesn't obscure the footer:

1. With Slide 3 displayed in slide view, use the Guides command on the View menu to turn on the guides.

2. Click anywhere in the object area once. PowerPoint surrounds the area with a shaded border, like this:

3. Point to the horizontal guide and hold down the left mouse button. Then drag upward until 2.00 appears in the guide's box.

4. Point to the top border of the object area and drag it upward until the border aligns with the horizontal guide.

Resizing and formatting slide areas

In addition to repositioning the title or object area of a slide, you can resize it by dragging its handles. Keep in mind that when you resize an area of a slide, the text inside it wraps to fit the area's new size. For example, a single line of text in a title area might wrap to two lines when you decrease the area's size. You can control whether text wraps or not by first selecting the area and choosing AutoShape from the Format menu. When the Format AutoShape dialog box appears, click the Text Box tab, deselect or select the Word Wrap Text In AutoShape option, and click OK. When you turn text wrapping off by deselecting this option, any text that does not fit within the area's frame continues beyond the frame's borders and, if necessary, even beyond the edges of the slide. Notice that you can also change the positioning of text within the box, adjust margins, and rotate the text 90° by selecting options in the Format AutoShape dialog box.

5. Click anywhere outside the slide to deselect the object area. Then turn off the guides. Here are the results:

6. Before we move on to the next chapter, check your work in slide sorter view. If everything looks good, give yourself a pat on the back for a job well done!

   Now you can put your skills and creative energy to work designing your own templates.

6

More About Electronic Presentations

After a discussion of equipment needs, we show you how to create dynamic presentations using transitions, text effects, and animation. Next, we cover different ways of adding interaction, such as hiding supporting information and branching to another presentation. Then we discuss taking a show on the road.

We use Paranormal Tours to show how to add special effects, draw on slides, and hide a slide with supporting information. We also show how to branch to a subordinate presentation and how to rehearse for a slide show using slide timings. Then we discuss the logistics of giving an electronic presentation and how to prepare to take a show on the road.

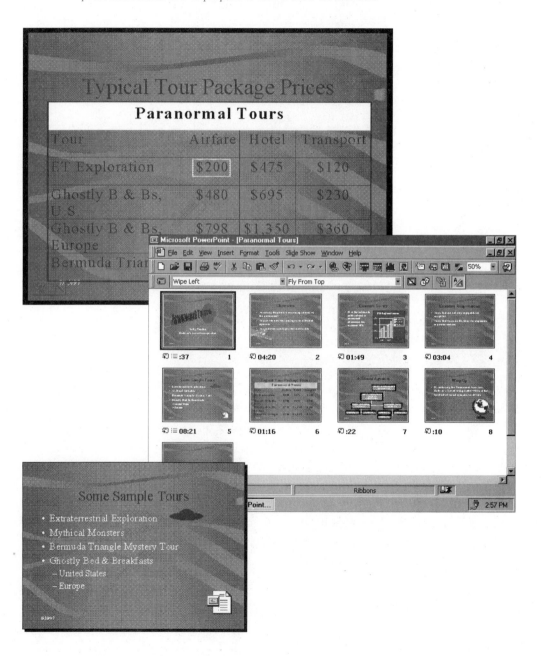

In Chapter 1, we introduced you to electronic slide shows and demonstrated how to run a presentation from your computer. In this chapter, we show you some of the more sophisticated things we can do with electronic slide shows, such as incorporate special effects and branch to another presentation. To round out the chapter, we also discuss equipment needs and the logistics of preparing for a presentation. And we show you how to take your slide shows on the road.

Electronic slide shows take more thought to prepare than overheads and 35mm slides—at least, the first slide show does—because we need to carefully consider the hardware aspects of the presentation. With overheads and 35mm slides, we usually show up for a presentation with a folder of transparencies or a carousel of slides, ready to dim the lights and get right to the point. Things aren't quite so simple with an electronic slide show. For one thing, the type of equipment we use varies with the size and nature of our audience, and for another, the potential exists for something to be missing or incompatible. For this reason, we start this section with a quick look at what we need in the way of hardware to give a successful electronic slide show.

Equipment for Electronic Slide Shows

The first thing to consider when we decide to develop an electronic slide show is how we plan to deliver the presentation. Will the audience be coming to us, or will we be doing the traveling? Will we be making the presentation on our own computer or someone else's? Whenever possible, it is wise to control as many variables as we can by developing the presentation on the computer we will be using to deliver the slide show. Otherwise, we can spend hours fine-tuning a dynamic presentation on a Pentium Pro with 64 MB of RAM for a conference in a distant city, only to find that the laptop provided by the conference organizers is a Pentium 75 with 16 MB of RAM. If we can't take the computer with us, we need to find out what kind of computer will be available so that we can make allowances for any major differences.

The computer →

The next question to consider is the size of the audience. Will we be making the presentation to a cozy group of less than five people around a conference table, a seminar of 30 people, or an auditorium of 100 or more? Although an intimate group might not mind crowding around a regular computer screen, for larger groups we will need a larger image. If we don't want to dim the lights and curtail audience interaction, we could use a 20-inch or larger monitor for a small seminar. But for addressing a room full of people, we will need either an LCD panel or an LCD projector to get our message across clearly.

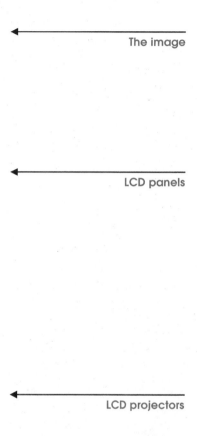

The image

LCD panels

LCD projectors

An LCD panel is a flat screen that plugs into a computer and displays a duplicate of the image we see on the computer's monitor. We lay the panel on an overhead projector to cast that image onto a standard slide screen. The resolution of the image is determined by the type of panel and by the brightness of the overhead projector. An active matrix panel with an overhead projector of 3000 to 4000 lumens is quite adequate for an audience of 50 or more people. Even with the highest resolution, though, the colors projected with the panel may not be the same as those on the computer's screen, so it's best not to use LCD panels in situations where precise colors are important (fashion design and interior decorating are good examples). An LCD projector operates on a similar principle, except that a light source and lens are built into the hardware. A good quality projector can project clear images for an audience of up to 300 people, but high quality projectors with active matrix displays and other image-enhancing features are expensive. Lower quality projectors cost less but may produce poor images that do nothing but annoy audiences.

For occasional use, we might be better off renting the necessary equipment, but then we need to be careful that all cables and other accessories are included with the primary hardware. If we are renting locally and transporting the equipment to the presentation site, we'll want to put everything together and test for compatibility before we leave, allowing time to return to the rental company for missing or replacement parts if necessary. If someone else is in charge of setting up the

Adjusting for the presentation output

When you change the output type for a presentation in the Page Setup dialog box, some of the elements that you define in one output type may shift when you display them in the new output type. For example, a graph may no longer be correctly sized for its slide after you switch output types from 35mm Slides to On-Screen Show. Always check every slide and make any necessary adjustments after you change the output type.

equipment, we should check with him or her ahead of time to prevent any misunderstandings about equipment needs.

Having passed on those few nuggets of wisdom, which we learned the hard way, let's fire up PowerPoint and talk more about creating and running electronic slide shows.

Using the Slide Show Tools

To help us control an electronic slide show, PowerPoint provides a variety of tools. As mentioned in Chapter 1, moving the mouse pointer during a slide show displays a button in the bottom left corner that we can click to open a menu of these tools. (We can also right-click to display the tools' object menu.) For example, by clicking the button and choosing the Go command, we can jump directly to a specific slide in the presentation. Let's spend a few moments familiarizing ourselves with some of the slide show tools:

1. Open Paranormal Tours and switch to slide show view. An animated block that is part of the Ribbons template arcs across your screen.

2. Move the mouse pointer over the screen, and when the slide show button appears, click it once to display this menu:

Meeting tools

When you run an electronic slide show during a meeting, you can rely on PowerPoint's Meeting Minder to help you record minutes or jot down action items. Simply choose Meeting Minder from the slide show object menu and use the tabs in the Meeting Minder dialog box accordingly. Any information you enter on the Meeting Minutes tab can be viewed via the Meeting Minder dialog box or by exporting the information to a Word document. When you record action items on the Action Items tab, PowerPoint adds an Action Items slide to the end of your presentation so that you and your colleagues can review the items. Like the meeting minutes, you can also export information on the Action Items tab to a Word document. To export minutes or action items to Word, click the Export button at the bottom of the Meeting Minder dialog box, select an Export Option, and then click Export Now. To take notes as you go through a slide show, choose Speaker Notes from the slide show object menu. If you type notes in the Speaker Notes dialog box, PowerPoint adds the notes to the presentation's notes pages. You can view the notes by switching to notes pages view or by opening the Speaker Notes dialog box during the slide show.

3. Choose Next to move to the next slide in the presentation.

4. Press the Page Up key once to remove the animated block from the right side of the screen, and again to move back to the first slide.

5. Right-click the slide and choose Go and then Slide Navigator to display this dialog box:

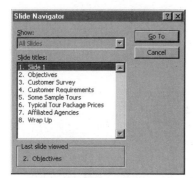

As you can see, PowerPoint identifies each slide by its number and its title. Because the title of the active slide is a WordArt object, it's listed simply as Slide 1.

6. Select Some Sample Tours, the fifth slide in the presentation, and click the Go To button to jump to Slide 5.

Jumping to another slide

7. Right-click again and choose Pointer Options and then Hide Always from the menu. The mouse pointer disappears.

Hiding the mouse pointer

8. Press Page Down to move to Slide 6.

9. Press Ctrl+A to redisplay the pointer. (You can also right-click and choose Arrow from the object menu.)

Redisplaying the mouse pointer

10. Right-click a final time and choose End Show to exit slide show view.

Running a Presentation Automatically

As we've already seen, we can manually run a slide show from our computer, clicking mouse buttons or pressing keys to progress from one slide to the next. But what if we want to move around the room as we deliver a presentation, or we want to be able to set the presentation in motion and then forget about it, as with point-of-purchase presentations? Instead of being tied to a mouse or keyboard, we can set up the slide show to automatically move from one slide to another. Let's automate the Paranormal Tours presentation. Before we do, however, we need to add a blank slide at the end of the presentation. Otherwise, when the slide show ends, Power-Point will abruptly switch us back to the view we were in before we started the show. Here goes:

Adding a blank slide

1. With the Paranormal Tours presentation open in slide view, move to Slide 8.

2. Click the New Slide button on the Standard toolbar, and when the New Slide dialog box appears, double-click the Blank autolayout (the last autolayout in the third row) to add a blank slide to the end of the presentation.

3. Next, switch to slide sorter view and choose Select All from the Edit menu to select all the slides in the presentation.

The Slide Transition button

4. Click the Slide Transition button on the Slide Sorter toolbar to display this dialog box:

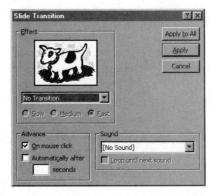

Setting the slide timings

5. We'll work with the Effect section of the dialog box in a moment. For now, click the Automatically After option in the Advance section, enter *10* in the Seconds edit box, and click Apply To All. PowerPoint indicates the timings you have set below each slide, as shown at the top of the facing page.

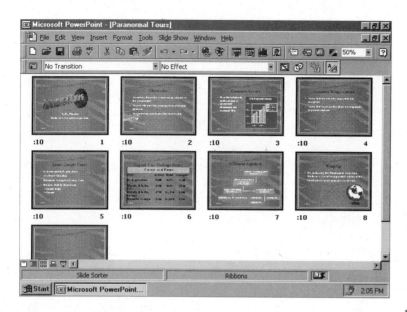

6. Now choose Set Up Show from the Slide Show menu to display this dialog box:

7. In the Advance Slides section, check that the Using Timings, If Present option is selected to activate the timings you set in the Slide Transition dialog box, and then click OK. Choose View Show from the Slide Show menu. PowerPoint switches to slide show view and displays Slide 1. After 10 seconds, it advances to Slide 2, then Slide 3, and so on.

More about the Set Up Show command

In the Show Type section of the Set Up Show dialog box, you can designate the type of slide show you want to set up. For a speaker-delivered presentation, leave the first option selected. For a self-running presentation (such as at a kiosk), select the second or third option. You can also set up the presentation to loop continuously until you press Esc, and you can run the presentation without narration or animation. If you want to show only specific slides during a slide show, enter the numbers of the slides in the From and To edit boxes in the Slides section and then click OK. When you click the Slide Show button to deliver the presentation, only the selected slides are displayed. Finally, you can change the pen color by selecting a new color in the Pen Color edit box. (We discuss the pen in more detail on page 141.)

8. Interrupt the show at any time by pressing Esc to return to slide sorter view.

Adding Special Effects

Setting up a presentation as an electronic slide show opens up the potential for using special effects that are not possible with overhead transparencies or 35mm slides. PowerPoint offers a wide range of special effects to choose from, including animation and sound. In this section, we'll discuss ways we can spruce up a presentation using transitions, text effects, and animation.

Adding Transitions

Transitions are visual and/or sound effects that we apply to a slide to help move the audience smoothly from one slide to the next, without the jerkiness associated with the replacement of one slide by another. Follow these steps to add transitions to all the slides of Paranormal Tours except the title slide:

1. In slide sorter view, check that all the slides are still selected. (If they're not, choose Select All from the Edit menu.) Then hold down the Shift key and click the title slide to deselect it. Now any commands you choose will affect all slides except the title slide.

2. Click the arrow to the right of the Slide Transition Effects box on the Slide Sorter toolbar, select Blinds Vertical from the drop-down list, and watch Slide 2 carefully as PowerPoint demonstrates the effect of the transition you have selected. Notice that PowerPoint displays a transition icon below the slides with transitions.

Testing transitions ⟶ 3. Click the title slide to select it. Then switch to slide show view and watch as PowerPoint runs the slide show with the specified transitions.

4. When PowerPoint reaches the blank slide, press Esc to switch back to slide sorter view, and experiment with other transition effects. For example, try applying a different effect to each slide—go a little crazy!

5. Next, select Slides 2 and 3, click the Slide Transition button on the Slide Sorter toolbar to display the Slide Transition dialog box, and in the Effect section, click the Slow option and then click Apply. Select Slide 1 and rerun the slide show with the transitions at this new speed.

◄——————————————
Changing the transition
speed

6. Now apply the Wipe Left transition to all the slides except the title slide, reset the speed to Fast, select Slide 1, and run through the slide show to test these transition settings.

As you've probably realized, it's easy to overdo transitions. Your audience will find these special effects less distracting if you stick to one kind of transition for all your slides and if you stick with the fast speed to keep them focused on the content of your presentation rather than its mechanics.

Adding Text Effects

Another way in which we can take advantage of our computer to raise our presentation above the level of a simple 35mm slide show is to add text effects to bulleted list slides. Text effects are animations that build the slide a bulleted item at a time. By using text effects, we can keep our audience focused on the point we are making right now, instead of allowing them to read ahead, perhaps diluting the impact of our message. Let's add a text effect to one of the slides in the Paranormal Tours presentation to see how they work:

1. In slide sorter view, select Slide 5, click the arrow to the right of the Text Preset Animation box, and select Fly From Left from the drop-down list. PowerPoint displays a text effect icon below Slide 5 to indicate that you have assigned a text effect to this slide.

2. Switch to slide show view to test the effect. The slide starts out with just its title and the UFO graphic, and then PowerPoint moves each bulleted item onto the slide in turn.

3. When the slide show moves to the next slide, return to slide sorter view by pressing Esc.

Moving the bulleted items in from the left is somewhat jarring because our eyes are accustomed to reading from left to right, not right to left. We can change the text effect on the toolbar, or we can make this and other changes in the Custom Animation dialog box. Follow these steps to display this dialog box:

1. Display Slide 5 in slide view. (To view the Custom Animation dialog box, you must be in slide view.)

2. Choose Custom Animation from the Slide Show menu.

3. In the Animation Order box of the Custom Animation dialog box, click 1.Text 2 and then click the Effects tab in the bottom half of the dialog box to display these options:

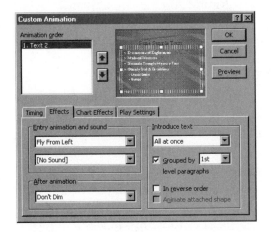

4. Change the animation setting to Fly From Right to make the text move in from the right instead of the left.

Dimming previous bulleted items

5. Click the arrow to the right of the After Animation box, select the fifth color, and then click OK.

6. Test your changes by switching to slide show view. Notice that PowerPoint now changes the color of existing bulleted items as it brings in a new item so that your audience's attention is always focused on the current point.

7. The 10-second display time for this slide now seems a little rushed. Switch to slide sorter view, select Slide 5, click the Slide Transition button, change the Automatically After setting in the Advance section to *20*, and then click Apply. In slide sorter view, the display setting for this slide changes from 10 to 20.

8. Select Slide 4, and switch to slide show view to test the transition to Slide 5, the text effect, and the transition to Slide 6.

Adding Animation

Animation effects are visual and/or sound effects that we apply to specific objects on a slide, such as the title. Power-Point provides an Animation Effects toolbar, which we can use to add animation to a presentation. To use the toolbar, we must display the presentation in slide view, and we must select an object on the current slide to animate. Follow these steps to add some animation effects to Paranormal Tours:

1. Display Slide 1 of Paranormal Tours in slide view.

2. Click the Animation Effects button on the Formatting toolbar to activate the Animation Effects toolbar.

The Animation Effects button

3. Select the *Paranormal Tours* title on Slide 1 (it should be surrounded by handles) and click the Camera Effect button on the Animation Effects toolbar.

The Camera Effect button

4. Select the subtitle, which consists of the two lines *Lilly Peushin* and *Gulliver's Travel Incorporated*, and click the Drop In button on the Animation Effects toolbar.

The Drop In button

5. Next, with the subtitle still selected, click the Custom Animation button on the Animation Effects toolbar. PowerPoint displays the Custom Animation dialog box shown here:

The Custom Animation button

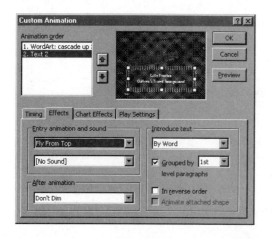

Previewing animation

To preview an animation effect while in slide view or outline view, choose Animation Preview from the Slide Show menu. The Color slide miniature appears in the presentation window, displaying the effects you selected for the current slide (including transitions and preset text animation effects). The Animation Preview command comes in handy when you want to see special effects in action without switching to slide show view.

Notice some of the settings in the dialog box, especially those on the Effects tab. Because you have selected the drop-in effect, the subtitle will appear word by word, as if dropped in place from above. Also notice the Animation Order setting at the top of the dialog box. Currently, the title on Slide 1 will appear first and the subtitle will appear second during a slide show. You can use the arrows next to the Animation Order box or the Animation Order drop-down list on the Animation Effects toolbar to change the order in which animated objects appear on a slide.

Changing animation order

6. If you have a sound card and speakers, click the down arrow to the right of the sound effects box, which is currently set to [No Sound]. Scroll the list of possible sounds, and select Whoosh. (If you have your own sound files, you can access them by selecting Other Sounds from the bottom of the drop-down list.)

Adding sound effects

7. Click OK in the Custom Animation dialog box to close the dialog box and implement your changes.

Let's experiment further with animation by adding an animation effect that will make the UFO graphic "fly" onto Slide 5. Follow these steps:

1. Move to Slide 5 and click the UFO graphic to select it.

2. Click the Custom Animation button on the Animation Effects toolbar and click the Timing tab, where PowerPoint lists Picture Frame 3 in the Slide Objects Without Animation box.

3. With Picture Frame 3 selected, click the Animate option in the Start Animation section. PowerPoint moves the selection to the Animation Order box above.

4. Click the Effects tab, and select the Fly From Top-Right animation option. (If you have a sound card, you can select a sound option as well.) Then click OK.

Now you're ready to test the animation effects we've added to Paranormal Tours:

1. Move to Slide 1 and click the Slide Show button.

PowerPoint Central

PowerPoint Central is a new feature of PowerPoint 97 that gives you an easy way to access multimedia clips and other information either from the installation disk (in the ValuPack) or from a page on Microsoft's Web site. To explore this feature, choose the PowerPoint Central command from the Tools menu. PowerPoint asks whether you want to update PowerPoint Central with the latest information. If you are not online, you can click No and still view the information stored on your hard drive. If you are online, you can click Yes to have PowerPoint download the latest files. On PowerPoint Central's main page, you can click the topics that interest you to get more information. Click the Free Stuff link to either see the items available on the installation disk or connect to the Microsoft Web site for additional free items. When you finish exploring, choose End Show from the File menu.

2. Run through the slide show, pressing Esc to return to slide view after you've seen the UFO graphic fly into place on Slide 5.

3. Close the Animation Effects toolbar.

Preparing Speaker-Controlled Presentations

The title of this section might surprise you. After all, aren't all presentations delivered by speakers? Not anymore. Presentation programs like PowerPoint now incorporate stand-alone capabilities that we can use to produce self-running presentations. We can mail these presentations to clients or use them as point-of-purchase displays or at trade shows. However, the majority of presentations are still delivered by a live human being, so in this section, we'll cover some of the special effects we can incorporate into a speaker-controlled electronic slide show. We'll also discuss how to rehearse for a presentation.

Adding Interaction

One measure of a good presentation is how well it delivers its message—whether it gets its point across. The design of the presentation itself obviously has a lot to do with its success, but a number of other factors come into play, such as the delivery style of the speaker and his or her ability to help the audience grasp the main thrust of the presentation. Also important is the speaker's ability (and willingness) to meet the audience's needs for clarification and more information. In this section, we discuss the PowerPoint features that enable us to maximize the chances that our audience will walk away from our electronic slide show having understood and accepted the message.

Drawing on the Slides

Although we have taken great pains to reduce the words on our slides to the minimum number needed to say what we want to say, during the course of a slide show, we might need to draw attention to a single word (or other element) on a slide. Just as we can mark up overhead transparencies with a felt-tip

Animating graphs and multimedia objects

To animate a graph using the Custom Animation dialog box, first display the slide with the graph you want to animate and then choose Custom Animation from the Slide Show menu. On the Timing tab, select the graph object in the Slide Objects Without Animation box and click the Animate option. Click the Chart Effects tab to select how the graph elements are introduced, to determine what type of animation and sound is used, and to decide what happens to each graph element after the animation effect is finished. (Remember, you can test your selections by clicking the Preview button.) If you have a multimedia object on a slide (such as a sound clip), you can animate that object by selecting it and clicking Animate on the Timing tab, and then clicking the Play Settings tab. Here, you can select options to control the sound, such as telling PowerPoint to continue playing the sound while displaying the slide show until it reaches a particular slide.

marker, we can mark up electronic slides with an on-screen "pen," and we don't even have to worry about cleaning up the mess afterward.

Suppose we decide that we want to emphasize some of the airfare prices on Slide 6 of the Paranormal Tours presentation. Follow these steps to see how to mark up a slide on-the-fly:

1. First, in slide sorter view, choose Select All from the Edit menu, click the Slide Transition button, deselect the Automatically After setting in the Advance section of the Slide Transition dialog box, and then click Apply To All so that you can manually move from slide to slide.

2. Now select Slide 6 and click the Slide Show button.

3. Click the right mouse button and choose Pen from the slide show object menu or press Ctrl+P. The pointer instantly takes the shape of a pen.

4. Move the pen pointer to the first item in the Airfare column, hold down the left mouse button, and draw a square or circle around $200. Then draw a square or circle around $566 at the bottom of the column. The slide now looks as shown here:

"Drill-down" files

If you have supporting information in a file created with another Windows application, you can access that information during a PowerPoint slide show by "drilling down" to it. For example, you can drill down to a report created in Word or an inventory list created in Access. The drill-down process requires OLE (object linking and embedding) and only works with applications that support OLE. To add a drill-down file to a presentation, you embed the file as an object. First choose Object from the Insert menu, and when the Insert Object dialog box appears, select the Create From File option and enter the complete path of the file in the File edit box. (If you don't know the path, click the Browse button and select the file in the Browse dialog box.) Next, select the Display As Icon option and click OK. The embedded object is then displayed on the current slide as an icon, and all you have to do to drill down to the file is double-click the icon. The originating application starts and displays the file in a window. To return to the presentation, choose Close & Return To *Presentation* (or a similar command) from the originating application's File menu.

Try changing the color of the pen's ink:

1. Click the right mouse button and choose Pointer Options and then Pen Color from the slide show object menu.

Changing the pen color

2. Select a different color from the drop-down list and then draw a few more squares or circles on Slide 6.

3. Click the right mouse button and choose Arrow from the slide show object menu or press Ctrl+A to restore the arrow pointer.

Returning to the arrow pointer

PowerPoint erases the pen ink as soon as you move to the next slide in the presentation. To erase the ink before moving on to the next slide, click the right mouse button and choose Screen and then Erase Pen from the slide show object menu, or simply press E.

Hiding Supporting Information

When someone in the audience requests clarification of a point we are making or questions our assumptions or conclusions, we will usually want to take the time to address their concerns before moving on. If we know the audience well, we can generally predict the kinds of questions they are likely to ask and can touch on those points in the presentation. But if we are unsure of the audience's level of knowledge about the topic or the focus of their interest, we probably won't want to clutter up the presentation with supporting information that the audience may not need. In that case, we might want to put the supporting information on hidden slides. Then if no questions are asked, we can simply skip over them. However, if the audience does need more information, we can display the hidden slides to qualify our statements or to provide the details.

In Chapter 3, we added a graph slide to the Paranormal Tours presentation with information about increasing public interest in paranormal phenomena. Suppose we want to hide this slide but keep it in the wings in case someone asks for data about the popularity of all things paranormal. Follow these steps to hide Slide 3:

1. Switch to slide sorter view and select Slide 3, the graph slide.

The Hide Slide button

2. Click the Hide Slide button on the Slide Sorter toolbar. PowerPoint indicates that the slide will be hidden by putting a slash through the slide number; it doesn't hide the slide in this view.

3. Select Slide 2 and switch to slide show view.

4. Click the left mouse button to move to the next slide. Power-Point skips over Slide 3 and displays Slide 4.

Displaying a hidden slide

5. Press P twice to return to Slide 2. Click the right mouse button and choose Go and then Hidden Slide from the object menu, or simply press H. PowerPoint displays the graph slide with its information about increased interest in the paranormal.

6. Press Page Up twice or press P twice to move back to Slide 2, and then click the left mouse button. PowerPoint takes you to Slide 4, skipping over the hidden slide once again.

7. Press Esc to return to slide sorter view, select Slide 3, and deselect the Hide Slide button.

Branching to a Subordinate Presentation

The ability to hide slides is useful when we want to have information available in case we need it to make a point. However, if we want to design a presentation for multiple audiences, a better alternative might be to build a core presentation and then incorporate other subordinate presentations that meet the needs of different groups. With some careful design work ahead of time, we can break down our presentations into reusable modules so that we can leverage our presentations in multiple directions.

As an example, suppose we want to be able to use the slides from the Sample Tours presentation in several other presentations. We can copy them from one presentation to another, but an alternate way of accomplishing the same thing without storing multiple copies of these slides in multiple presentations is to embed the file in each of the presentations where these slides are needed. Follow these steps to embed the Sample Tours presentation in the Paranormal Tours presentation:

1. Display Slide 5 of Paranormal Tours in slide view and choose Object from the Insert menu to open the Insert Object dialog box shown below. (The Object command is not available in slide sorter view.)

Embedding one presentation in another

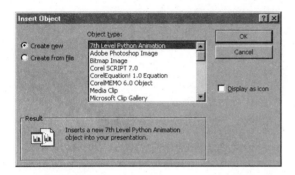

2. Scroll the Object Type list and select Microsoft PowerPoint Presentation. Then click the Create From File option, click an insertion point at the end of the entry in the File edit box, and type *Sample Tours.ppt*.

3. Now click the Display As Icon option and click the Change Icon button to display this dialog box:

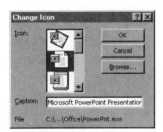

4. The selected icon is fine, but let's delete the caption. Select the text in the Caption edit box, press Delete, and click OK twice to return to slide view, where PowerPoint has inserted a tiny icon.

5. Move, size, and crop the icon until it looks like the one shown on the next page (see page 95 for information about cropping).

Interactive presentations

You can create a menu of presentations for the viewer to choose from by embedding several presentations on a blank slide and not selecting the Display As Icon option in the Insert Object dialog box. When you don't select the Display As Icon option, a thumbnail of each embedded presentation's first slide appears on the current slide. Using the mouse, the thumbnails can be resized and repositioned adjacent to descriptions of each presentation. (Use the Text Box button on the Drawing toolbar to add descriptions.) For example, you can embed a presentation about each of several products in a general sales presentation. Viewers can then double-click a thumbnail to watch a presentation about the product that interests them.

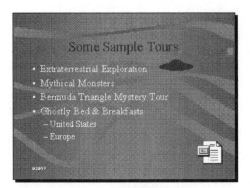

6. Next, with the icon selected, choose Action Settings from the Slide Show menu to display this dialog box:

Interactive objects

As you saw when you embedded the Sample Tours presentation in the Paranormal Tours presentation, the Action Settings dialog box allows you to make objects on a slide interactive. Take a look at some of the other options in this dialog box. (You must select an object on a slide in slide view before you can choose the Action Settings command.) You can specify different actions to take place when you click a specific object on a slide. For example, you can select the title of Slide 1, choose Action Settings from the Slide Show menu, select the Hyperlink To option, and then select Last Slide from the drop-down list to jump to the last slide in the presentation when you click the title of Slide 1 during a slide show. (You can also create hyperlinks to other presentations, files, or Web addresses.) Some of the other options in the dialog box let you play a sound or run an application when the selected object is clicked.

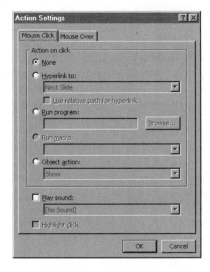

7. Select Object Action, and with Show selected in the drop-down list, click OK.

Let's see how PowerPoint handles branching to a subordinate presentation:

1. Switch to slide show view and click the left mouse button until all the bulleted items and the UFO graphic are displayed. Then click the presentation icon. PowerPoint branches to the Sample Tours presentation and displays Slide 1.

2. Click the left mouse button four times to step through the remaining Sample Tours slides, and click it a fifth time to return to Slide 5 of Paranormal Tours.

3. Move the pointer away from the presentation icon, and click again to move on to Slide 6 of Paranormal Tours.

Preparing for Delivery

Some people can stand up before a group and deliver an impromptu speech that nevertheless sounds eloquent and well-reasoned. The rest of us must practice, practice, practice. Even if you are an experienced speaker, you will probably want to make sure you are prepared to handle the glitches that can arise with an electronic presentation. A tiny setback can be explained to a sympathetic audience and circumvented; an accumulation of setbacks can spell disaster.

The key to avoiding embarrassment is adequate rehearsal. With electronic slide shows, rehearsing takes two forms: one involving the pacing of your presentation, and the other involving logistics. We'll look at both forms in this section.

PowerPoint Rehearsals

The hallmarks of a planned presentation are that it starts on time, ends on time, and proceeds at an easy pace in between. It accommodates questions and relevant tangents but nevertheless sticks to the topic at hand and tells the audience members what they need to know. If we have been allocated 45 minutes to give a presentation, and, using a formula of about 2 minutes per slide, we create an electronic slide show of 25 slides, we will probably be uncomfortable if we get to the last slide with 20 minutes to kill. Conversely, if we are only on Slide 20 when our time is up and we have to rush our conclusion, we will probably kick ourselves for not having allowed enough time to hammer home our message.

PowerPoint can't create a powerful presentation for us, but it can help us ensure that the presentation is correctly paced. You have seen how to use the Automatically After setting in the Advance section of the Slide Transition dialog box to have PowerPoint move automatically from one slide to another.

Action buttons

PowerPoint's action buttons let you create hyperlinks to other slides, presentations, movies, and so on. To add a button to the current slide, choose Action Buttons from the Slide Show menu and select a button from the available palette. Then drag a frame in the area of the slide where you want the button to appear. The Action Settings dialog box automatically appears so that you can assign an action to the button.

Instead of entering an arbitrary number of seconds for this setting as we did earlier, we can have PowerPoint record how long each slide stays on the screen while we rehearse the presentation, and we can then use the recorded time for each slide as its Automatically After setting. This process not only gives us an idea of how long the total presentation is (when we proceed without audience interruption) but means that we can use PowerPoint's automatic advancement through the slides to keep us on track and on time.

To record the slide timings for the Paranormal Tours presentation, follow these steps:

The Rehearse Timings button

1. Switch to slide sorter view and click the Rehearse Timings button on the Slide Sorter toolbar. PowerPoint switches to slide show view and displays this Rehearsal dialog box in the bottom right corner of the slide:

The clock on the left shows the accumulated time for the entire presentation, and the clock on the right shows the time for the current slide.

2. Say a few pertinent sentences about the title slide of the presentation (be sure to click the left mouse button to display the title and subtitle), and then click the mouse button or the right-pointing arrow in the dialog box to move on to Slide 2. The clock on the right then resets to 0 and begins timing the second slide.

3. Repeat step 2 for the remaining slides. If you need to start over for a given slide, click the Repeat button in the Rehearsal dialog box. If you need to pause, click the button with the two vertical bars. (Click it again to resume.)

4. When you reach the blank slide at the end of the presentation, press the Esc key. PowerPoint displays this message box:

Slide Meter

After you have recorded the slide timings for a presentation, you can run through the presentation again and use the Slide Meter to gauge your progress. To activate the meter, display Slide 1 of your presentation in slide show view, click the right mouse button, and choose Slide Meter from the slide show object menu. By default, the Slide Meter appears in the bottom right corner of the slide, but you can drag it to any location on the slide. The timer at the top of the meter shows the elapsed time for the displayed slide, and the timer in the middle shows the elapsed time for all the slides up to and including the displayed slide. The progress bar at the bottom of the Slide Meter compares your rehearsed time to your current time and indicates whether you need to slow down or speed up.

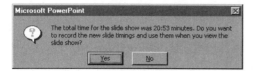

5. Make a note of the total time taken for the presentation, click Yes to enter the slide timings for each slide in the Slide Transition dialog box, and click Yes once more to redisplay slide sorter view, where the slides now look as shown here:

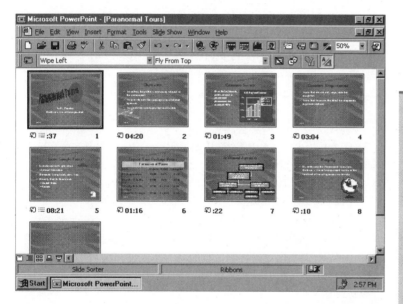

If the total presentation time is too long, we can talk less while each slide is displayed, or we can look for ways to cut the number of slides. If the time is too short, we can talk more while each slide is displayed, or we can add slides. Either way, we can repeat the rehearsal process to enter new timings for each slide until we get the pace of the presentation just right. Then we need to switch from manual to automatic advancement in the Slide Show dialog box, like this:

1. Choose Set Up Show from the Slide Show menu.

2. In the Set Up Show dialog box, check that Using Timings, If Present in the Advance Slides section is selected and then click OK.

Custom slide shows

If you plan to give an electronic slide show to several different audiences and you need to vary the presentation slightly in each case, you can use the Custom Shows command to create a custom slide show to which you can branch off during the presentation. Simply choose Custom Shows from the Slide Show menu, click the New button in the Custom Shows dialog box, and enter a name for the show in the Define Custom Show dialog box. Then select the slides you want to include in the custom show and click the Add button. You can use the arrow buttons to rearrange the order of the slides. When you are done, click OK to return to the Custom Shows dialog box, where you can see a preview of the new show by clicking the Show button. To run a custom show from slide show view, choose Go and then Custom Show from the slide show object menu, and then select the show you want.

3. Switch to slide show view and rehearse the presentation one more time while PowerPoint runs the slide show.

Pausing the slide show and blanking the screen

If PowerPoint advances to the next slide while we are talking, we can press the S key to pause the slide show and then press either the B key to turn the screen black or the W key to turn it white while we finish what we are saying. Pressing S again resumes the show. (The Pause and Black Screen commands can also be accessed by choosing Screen from the slide show object menu.) If we finish talking before the end of a slide's allocated display time—for example, if we allowed time for questions and there are none—we can always click the left mouse button to manually advance to the next slide. (Remember that either of these pacing adjustments will increase or decrease the total length of the presentation.)

Manually advancing an automatic slide show

Taking Care of Logistics

If you will be running your presentation under controlled conditions—in your own office using your own computer, for example, or in a familiar auditorium with equipment you have used before—you can probably skip this section. Otherwise, you should know that Murphy has a field day with electronic slide shows and that sooner or later "anything that can go wrong will go wrong." The only way to thwart Murphy's Law is to prepare adequately.

The first area to troubleshoot is the presentation equipment. Make sure you have everything you need and know how to put it together. Locate the electrical outlets in the room, set up the equipment, and check that everything is working. If someone else is in charge of setup, check in advance that they know exactly what you need, but still make a point of arriving early and, if necessary, turn on the system—just to be sure.

Next, check the setup from the point of view of the audience. If you are using a projector, make sure it is the correct distance from the screen and focused to produce the sharpest image. If you are using a microphone, check its volume. Check where the light switches/dimmers are and make sure any lights that can't be dimmed do not shine directly on the screen. Also check that you can sit or stand to the side of the computer

Emergency accessories

Before you strike off on your own to give an electronic slide show, remember to pack a few accessories in case of emergency:

- A checklist of all the items you need for a successful presentation (including such things as speaker's notes and/or handouts, computer cables, mouse pointer, remote control, software and extra disks, and a sound unit/amplifier)
- Overhead transparencies or back-up slides
- Small flashlight and extra batteries (so that you can find the keyboard or your notes with the lights dimmed)
- Screwdriver and small wrench (in case you have connector problems), and extra bulbs for the overhead or LCD projector (in case one burns out)
- Extension cord (so that you can reach a distant outlet)
- A backup copy of your presentation

table so that you and your audience can see each other but you can also view the screen.

If you are not using your own computer, load your presentation from disk onto the computer's hard drive ahead of time. If possible, rehearse your presentation in the room and with the equipment and lighting you will actually use.

And in case of disaster, duplicate your electronic slide show as a set of overhead transparencies and handouts and bring them with you so that you can switch to this tried-and-true format if necessary. The show must go on!

Taking a Show on the Road

Sometimes we need to deliver a presentation without knowing whether the computer that will be used has PowerPoint installed on it. For these occasions, PowerPoint has a feature that ensures we have everything we need to make the electronic slide show a success. Aptly named, the Pack And Go Wizard steps us through a series of dialog boxes, asking questions about the presentation and any additional files it includes.

The Pack And Go Wizard

Let's use the Pack And Go Wizard right now to pack up the Paranormal Tours presentation so that we can run it on a computer that does not have PowerPoint:

1. Insert a blank disk and the PowerPoint installation disk, which you will need for this example.

2. With Paranormal Tours displayed on your screen, choose Pack And Go from the File menu to display this dialog box:

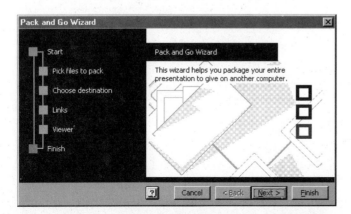

3. Click Next, check that Active Presentation is selected, and then click Next again to display the dialog box shown here:

Here, you can select a disk drive or click Choose Destination and either type the path where you want the files stored on your hard drive or click Browse to navigate to the destination you want.

4. Select the appropriate floppy drive letter and then click Next to display this dialog box:

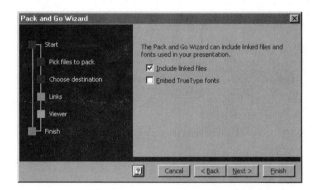

If you select Include Linked Files, you will bring any linked files and can access them from the destination computer. If you click Embed TrueType Fonts, the wizard will embed fonts used in the presentation to ensure that text is correctly displayed if some fonts are not installed on the destination computer.

Presentation conferencing

If you need to give a presentation, but not all of the participants can be together in one room, you may want to explore PowerPoint's presentation conferencing feature. This feature allows the speaker to give a presentation either over a network or via the Internet. To use presentation conferencing, all participants of the presentation (the speaker and the audience) must work through the Presentation Conference Wizard by first choosing the Presentation Conference command from the Tools menu. PowerPoint then walks each participant through the steps of setting up the conference. Any multimedia objects (such as sound or video) or embedded objects (such as a graph created in Microsoft Graph) on the slides cannot be seen or heard by the audience when using presentation conferencing. For more information about this feature, you can check online help.

5. Leave just the Include Linked Files option selected for this exercise and then click Next to display this dialog box:

If the destination computer is running Windows 95 or NT but does not have PowerPoint installed, you can tell the Pack And Go Wizard to include the PowerPoint Viewer. (If the destination computer is running Windows 3.1, you will need to load the PowerPoint Viewer in a separate process—see the tip below.)

PowerPoint Viewer

6. Select Viewer For Windows 95 Or NT and click Next.

7. Read the final dialog box and then click Finish. The Pack And Go Wizard packs up all the necessary files, including the PowerPoint Viewer, on the disk. (If you have not inserted the installation disk, the wizard will prompt you for it.)

8. When a message box announces that the Pack And Go Wizard has finished, click OK and exit PowerPoint.

Now let's run the presentation to simulate delivering it on a destination computer. Follow the steps on the next page.

Running a presentation on a Windows 3.1 computer

As we mentioned, you need to install the PowerPoint Viewer in a separate process if you are going to run a presentation on a Windows 3.1 computer. After you have used the Pack And Go Wizard to pack up the presentation—without the viewer—on one disk, copy the viewer to a different disk. Open Windows Explorer, insert the PowerPoint installation disk, navigate to the Valupack\Ppt4view folder, and copy the folder to the disk. To run the viewer on the Windows 3.1 computer, insert the disk containing the viewer, choose Run from Program Manager's File menu, type *a:\ppt4view\vsetup* in the Command Line edit box, and click OK. Follow the instructions to install PowerPoint Viewer on the hard drive. Then insert the disk containing the presentation and follow steps similar to steps 1 through 3 on page 154. Finally, run PowerPoint Viewer by double-clicking its icon, select the presentation, and click Show.

Running a presentation on
another computer

1. Create a new folder on your hard drive from which to run the presentation.

2. Choose Run from the Windows 95 Start menu, then type *A:\Pngsetup*, and click OK.

3. In the Pack And Go Setup dialog box, select the destination folder you created in step 1 on the hard drive and click OK.

4. Click OK in the message box that warns you that the viewer won't work in Windows 3.1, and then click Yes to run the show.

Congratulations! You have now completed your Quick Course in PowerPoint. By now, you should feel comfortable with all the components of PowerPoint. With the basics you have learned here, together with the Help feature and the sample presentations that come with the program, you can tackle the creation of some pretty sophisticated presentations. Good luck!

Index